Coordination Games

Complementarities and Macroeconomics

This book studies the implications of macroeconomic complementarities for aggregate behavior. The presentation is intended to introduce Ph.D. students into this subfield of macroeconomics and to serve as a reference for more advanced scholars. The initial sections of the book cover the basic framework of complementarities and provide a discussion of the experimental evidence on the outcome of coordination games. The subsequent sections discuss the implications of complementarities for macroeconomics. The topics covered include economies with production complementarities, search models, imperfectly competitive product markets, and the roles of government in resolving and creating coordination problems. The presentation goes into the new models and treats them as a structurally related literature. The discussion brings together theory and quantitative analy

Russell W. Cooper is
previ
Iowa.
of un
paper
econo
Revie
Econ
nomi
Econ

Coordination Games

Complementarities and Macroeconomics

RUSSELL W. COOPER

CAMBRIDGE
UNIVERSITY PRESS

PUBLISHED BY THE PRESS SYNDICATE OF THE UNIVERSITY OF CAMBRIDGE
The Pitt Building, Trumpington Street, Cambridge CB2 1RP, United Kingdom

CAMBRIDGE UNIVERSITY PRESS
The Edinburgh Building, Cambridge CB2 2RU, UK   http://www.cup.cam.ac.uk
40 West 20th Street, New York, NY 10011-4211, USA http://www.cup.org
10 Stamford Road, Oakleigh, Melbourne 3166, Australia

First published 1999

Printed in the United States of America

Typeset in Times Roman 10.5/13, on Miles 33 [EW]

A catalog record for this book is available from the British Library.

Library of Congress Cataloging-in-Publication Data
Cooper, Russell W., 1955—
Coordination games : Complementarities and macroeconomics / Russell W. Cooper.
p. cm.
Includes bibliographical references and index.
ISBN 0-521-57017-4 (hardbound)–ISBN 0-521-57896-5 (pbk)
1. Macroeconomics–Mathematical models. 2. Equilibrium
(Economics)–Mathematical models. I. Title.
HB172.5.C69   1998
339'.01'5118–dc21   98-20151
                        CIP

ISBN 0 521 57017 4 hardback
ISBN 0 521 57896 5 paperback

Contents

Preface

The goal of this book is to provide a synthesis of research on the topic of complementarities in macroeconomics. Its primary goal is to isolate the various sources of complementarity and then to explore their implications for the behavior of macroeconomies. The success of this approach is seen through the numerous theoretical and empirical applications of the basic structure inherent in model economies built upon the macroeconomic complementarities structure.

As this is principally a book about applications in macroeconomics, it has been necessary to leave aside a number of topics that relate to the implications of complementarities for other branches of economics, such as industrial organization. Still, the reader interested in applications outside macroeconomics ideally will find the more general discussion of models of complementarities as well as the presentation of experimental evidence of some value.

The first two chapters as well as the next section of this Preface focus on general issues arising in models of complementarities, thus providing a framework for the more applied analysis that will follow. In particular, the first two chapters discuss experimental evidence on coordination games and theories of selection and put forth a general model of macroeconomic complementarities.

The remaining chapters explore applications of the general structure by investigating particular channels of interactions across agents. This includes the study of economies in which (i) externalities are present in the technology of the individual agent, (ii) markets are imperfectly competitive, (iii) agents come together through a search process and (iv) information is imperfect. As we shall see, all of these deviations from the standard general equilibrium model of Arrow and Debreu can give rise to macroeconomic complementarities.

The structure of the presentation has two important aspects. First, as much as possible, I have tried to blend theory and quantitative analysis. This is mainly apparent in the more applied chapters, where specific models of complementarity have been "taken to the data." This blending of theory and quantitative analysis is important since ultimately models are evaluated in terms of their ability to "match" observations. Further, the presentation makes clear that even though a model with complementarities is more complex than, say, a representative agent structure, quantitative analyses are possible. In fact, one might speculate that our ability to deal quantitatively with dynamic strategic interactions between heterogeneous agents will only enrich the set of models with complementarities we can quantitatively investigate.

Second, each chapter is organized around a core model that is analyzed in some detail. In addition, extensions of the basic model are examined, though in less detail. The idea is to provide a sense of the literature through a core model.

WHAT ARE COORDINATION GAMES?

This book studies a very special but rich class of games, called *coordination games*. These games have a number of distinct characteristics that make them quite interesting in many areas of economic research. As this is essentially a book about macroeconomics, our focus will be mainly on macroeconomic examples and implications of coordination games for the aggregate economy.

In contrast to many strategic situations, coordination games do not rest solely upon conflict between players. Instead, confidence and expectations are critical elements in the types of coordination games that we will study. In particular, the possibility of coordination failures, arising from self-fulfilling pessimistic beliefs, is observed in equilibrium. The resulting inefficiencies are, in turn, quite interesting in a variety of macroeconomic contexts.

To motivate this, we begin purposefully with a game that is outside macroeconomics. Consider the fascinating example discussed by Schelling [1960] in which two individuals must independently decide where to locate. Further, to emphasize the gains to coordination, suppose that these players achieve positive utility only if their choices agree. So, the players gain utility if and only if they choose the same location. Clearly, the gains from interaction are derived solely from coordination rather than conflict. In this setting, multiple noncooperative equilibria easily emerge since all that matters is that players make similar choices. Still, there is a nontrivial problem here: where should the players locate given that they must act independently?

These types of situations can be embellished by supposing that certain outcomes, in which players take the same action, bring higher payoffs than others. So, in the location problem, suppose that there are two locations, A and B. Further, assume that players are better off locating at point B than not locating at the same point, but they are even better off if they locate at point A. Thus, there are gains to coordinating at any point and further gains to coordinating at point A instead of point B.

For this game, there are again multiple noncooperative equilibria. In one both players go to A and in the other both go to location B. In this situation, the multiple equilibria are Pareto-ranked. Still, a coordination failure can easily arise: in the equilibrium in which all players locate at point B, all players would be better off if they could coordinate their choices and thus go to location A. Despite this, the outcome when both go to location B seems to qualify as a legitimate noncooperative outcome since both players are best responding to the (anticipated) action of the other.

This book is devoted to the study of environments where coordination games naturally emerge. Our focus is on the theoretical basis for these coordination problems and the likely outcome in these strategic situations. These games have a number of properties that make them particularly applicable to macroeconomics and of special interest to game theorists as well.

First, as in the preceding location example, coordination games may exhibit multiple *Pareto-ranked equilibria*. This gives some content to the theme, often expressed in macroeconomics, that an economy may be "stuck" at an inefficient equilibrium. While all agents in the economy understand that the outcome is inefficient, each, acting independently, is powerless to coordinate the activities of other agents to reach a Pareto-preferred equilibrium. So, from this perspective, a depression in aggregate economic activity arises when the economy falls into the trap of a low activity level Nash equilibrium. In addition, all of the equilibria may be Pareto-dominated by some other feasible outcome, as in the familiar *prisoner's dilemma game.* To this degree, externalities are not internalized by individual agents.

Second, the nature of the strategic interactions underlying the multiple equilibria of the game has implications for the behavior of economies built around the repeated play of coordination games. In particular, the actions of players in coordination games are strategic complements, implying that increases in the level of activity of other agents create an incentive for increased activity by the remaining agent. These interactions may exist both intra- and intertemporally and are interesting for macroeconomics as they generate the positive correlation in activity levels across agents and persistence over time which are characteristic of macroeconomic time series.

Third, these games have captured the attention of game theorists, leading to powerful results on the nature of equilibria for coordination games and the process of attaining an equilibrium outcome. Developing these more game theoretic topics requires us to explore a class of games, termed *supermodular games,* into which the coordination games emphasized in macroeconomics neatly fit. This is taken up in Chapter 2, while subsequent chapters investigate these themes by analyzing macroeconomic applications in detail.

This overview introduces coordination games through a simple example. We use this example to be more specific about the themes of this book. Moreover, before delving into the details of conditions under which multiple equilibria and thus coordination failures can occur, it is useful to address a prior concern about evidence on outcomes of coordination games. Thus, Chapter 1 builds upon the simple example to provide a discussion of experimental evidence on coordination games and theories of selection that have been proposed for this type of strategic interaction.

AN EXAMPLE

Consider a game between two players, A and B, both of whom provide effort in a production process.[1] Assume that player i receives a payoff of $2c_i - e_i$ from consumption (c_i) and effort (e_i), $i = 1, 2$. Further suppose that

---

1. This is motivated by the discussion in Bryant [1983], which we return to in some detail in Chapter 2.

per capita consumption equals $\min(e_1, e_2)$ and that only two effort levels are feasible, i.e., $e_i \in \{1, 2\}$. The payoff matrix for this coordination game is given by

		Player B	
		1	2
Player	1	1, 1	1, 0
A	2	0, 1	2, 2

Coordination game

There are two pure strategy Nash equilibria in this simultaneous move game, the strategy profiles $\{1, 1\}$ and $\{2, 2\}$, as well as a mixed strategy equilibrium in which each player selects action 1 with probability 1/2. These are Nash equilibria because each agent is acting optimally given the choice of the other. Note, though, that the $\{2, 2\}$ equilibrium Pareto-dominates both the $\{1, 1\}$ equilibrium and the mixed strategy equilibrium. In this sense, neither the pure strategy equilibrium at $\{1, 1\}$ nor the mixed strategy equilibrium is socially optimal.

The multiplicity of Nash equilibria here has nothing to do with the large number of equilibria that emerge in games of incomplete information. That is, the various equilibria are not a consequence of assumptions regarding the structure of beliefs off an equilibrium path since the coordination game assumes complete information. Further, the equilibria of this coordination game are regular (strict) in that under small perturbations of the payoffs, the set of pure strategy equilibria does not change.[2]

Instead, the multiplicity of equilibria, and thus the possibility of a Pareto-inferior equilibrium, derives from agents' inability to coordinate their choices in this strategic environment. As a consequence, realized equilibrium outcomes that are Pareto-suboptimal relative to other equilibria, such as $\{1, 1\}$, are often termed *coordination failures*.

A key element in the structure of this game concerns the extra payoff a player receives from taking a "high" action (strategy 2 in the game) as a function of the action chosen by the other player. In the preceding coordination game, the increased payoff for player A to switching from

---

2. That is, smaller variations in the payoffs of the game do not result in large changes in the number of equilibria. This contrasts to the sensitivity of equilibria in the normal form representations of signaling games.

action 1 to action 2 is -1 when B chooses 1 but is 1 when B chooses 2. Thus, higher action by player B increases the marginal return to higher action by player A. This property of positive feedback, often termed *strategic complementarity,* is central to the characterization of coordination games and will form the centerpiece of the analysis that follows.

Further, the game exhibits *positive spillovers* in that the payoffs of one player increase as the action chosen by the other increases. In particular, if player A chooses 2, then A's payoff is higher when B selects strategy 2 than if B selects strategy 1. Note that this property of a positive spillover measures the effect of B's action on A's payoff given A's action, in contrast to the concept of strategic complementarity, which is informative about the payoff consequences of changes in A's action as a function of B's action.

An important issue in this and other coordination games is the selection of an equilibrium outcome. For this coordination game, what outcome will arise? One might argue that the Pareto-dominant Nash equilibrium in which both players select 2 is a natural focal point.[3] Alternatively, the choice of strategy 2 is, for both players, "risky" in that if their opponent does not also select action 2, the payoff loss is 1, while there is no uncertainty from choosing strategy 1.[4] From this perspective, the likely outcome might be {1, 1} since this leaves players exposed to no risk whatsoever. To pursue these themes in more detail, Chapter 1 summarizes experimental evidence on coordination games and some theories of equilibrium selection.

For macroeconomics, when the strategy, i.e., effort levels, are ordered, the coordination game is a framework in which equilibria with low levels of economic activity can arise. To provide this macroeconomic perspective, we will discuss a number of economic examples that can be represented as coordination games in subsequent chapters.

These economies, of course, must deviate from the Arrow–Debreu model of perfect competition with complete contingent markets. In that model, the choices of individual agents are completely coordinated through the market mechanism: there are no missing markets. Further, traders are costlessly matched by the auctioneer. Finally, in the spirit of perfect competition, no traders have any influence on prices. The examples that

3. This point appears most recently in Harsanyi and Selten [1988, p. 356], who stress the role of payoff dominance in selecting an equilibrium outcome. In this game, Harsanyi and Selten would then argue that the {2, 2} outcome was focal as a result of its payoff dominance.
4. Harsanyi and Selten provide a formal treatment of strategic uncertainty, which they term *risk dominance* and apply to games with multiple Nash equilibria which are not Pareto-ordered. Their concepts and arguments are presented later.

we explore provide insights into the roles of externalities in the production process, matching and imperfect competition as important sources of distortions leading to coordination failures.

As described in the next chapters, one can associate levels of economic activity with the strategies of the coordination game and discover that the multiple equilibria correspond to high and low activity levels in which equilibria with high levels of activity Pareto-dominate. Still, the economy can become stuck in a low level, Pareto-inferior equilibrium, since each agent, acting alone, cannot coordinate the activities of all agents.

Besides the multiplicity of equilibria, coordination games provide insights into other macroeconomic phenomena. In particular, as a result of the nature of the strategic interaction across agents, there is a natural propagation mechanism inherent in these games. Changes in the underlying parameters describing the payoffs to one agent (i.e., shocks to one player) lead to similar responses in the behavior of all agents. In particular, if a shock to one agent leads that agent to choose a higher level of activity, then other agents will also choose higher levels of activity. In this case, a shock that is not common to all agents will lead to positive comovement in activity levels economywide, a feature that is important in business cycles. Further, in dynamic versions of these models, these shocks can be propagated over time as well.

PROGRAMS AND RESEARCH UPDATES

Research is an ongoing process. By the time this book is published, a number of new advances will undoubtedly have been made. It is useful then to have a source of information on research in this area.

Further, the discussion in this book often rests upon numerical results, in the form of either simulated games or simulations of simple aggregate economies. The interested reader might benefit from access to these programs. To facilitate that access, I have created a Website which will contain research updates as well as relevant computer programs. The address is http://econ.bu.edu/faculty/cooper/macrocomp.

THANKS

A special debt is owed to Douglas Gale, whose initiatives got this project started. Discussions with Douglas on the nature of the material and the structure of its presentation immensely improved the product.

As the reader will notice, this book draws heavily upon my joint work in the area of complementarities. Whatever the value of these contributions, I am certainly indebted to the long list of coauthors, critics and discussants who, over the years, have enriched my understanding of these issues including Andrew John, Thomas Ross, John Haltiwanger, Douglas Gale, Robert Forsythe, Douglas DeJong, Satyajit Chatterjee, B. Ravikumar, Alok Johri, Joao Ejarque, Dean Corbae, Jess Benhabib, Costas Azariadis, Roger Farmer, Jang-Ting Guo, Christophe Chamley, Jon Eaton, Nobuhiro Kiyotaki, Randall Wright, Peter Howitt, Peter Diamond, Robert Hall, Olivier Blanchard, Hubert Kempf, Pierre Cahuc, John Bryant, Walter Heller and John van Huyck. A special thanks to Joyce Cooper and Jon Willis for their careful reading of this manuscript.

Parts of this book have been presented as short courses in a variety of institutions, including the Bank of Portugal; Federal Reserve Bank of Richmond; joint Finnish Ph.D. program in Tampera, Finland; Tel Aviv University; University of Paris I; University of Toulouse; University of Aix-Marseille; University of Copenhagen and UCLA. I am grateful to these institutions for hosting my courses and to the participants for giving their suggestions and encouragement.

Financial support from the National Science Foundation, the Social Sciences and Humanities Research Council and the CNRS for the research that underlies this book is certainly appreciated. Finally, I am grateful to Cambridge University Press for its support and patience during the volume's long preparation.

1 Experimental Evidence and Selection

The introductory discussion provides an example to illustrate the possibility of coordination failure due to the presence of multiple Pareto-ranked Nash equilibria. Of course, as remarked earlier, whether coordination failures actually occur depends on the selection of an outcome from the set of Nash equilibria. If, for instance, the Pareto-dominant Nash equilibrium is a natural focal point, as suggested, for example, by Harsanyi–Selten [1988], then understanding the macroeconomic implications of coordination failures would be somewhat less interesting.

This chapter first reviews some recent experimental evidence that bears directly on equilibrium selection in coordination games.[1] The evidence both concerns results on equilibrium selection and provides some insights into the process of equilibration. The second part of this chapter describes a variety of selection theories that bear directly on coordination games.

One conclusion of the experimental evidence is that coordination problems are not a pure theoretical curiosity. In particular, coordination failures are routinely observed in experimental games.

EXPERIMENTAL EVIDENCE

The discussion of experimental evidence is partitioned into three parts. First, evidence from simple coordination games is presented. Given the frequency of coordination failures observed in these experiments, further

---

1. This discussion draws heavily upon Cooper et al. [1994].

1

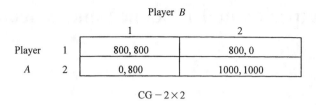

Figure 1.1

treatments which explore possible remedies to coordination problems, such as preplay communication, are presented.

Baseline Experiments

As a starting point, consider the coordination game in Figure 1.1. This game was the focus of a study of experimental coordination games by Cooper, DeJong, Forsythe and Ross [1992]. In this game, there are two pure strategy Nash equilibria, $\{1, 1\}$ and $\{2, 2\}$, and a mixed strategy equilibrium. The equilibrium in which both players choose strategy 2 clearly Pareto-dominates the other equilibria. Thus, arguments for Pareto domination as a selection criterion imply that the $\{2, 2\}$ outcome should be observed in the play of this game.

An interesting aspect of this game is the riskiness of the strategy profile that leads to the Pareto-dominant Nash equilibrium at $\{2, 2\}$. In particular, if player B has a significant doubt (in this case if B assigns a probability less than .8) that player A will choose to play 2, his best action is to choose 1. By symmetry, the same goes for A. So, if there is significant doubt in the minds of the players about the likely action of their opponent, they might choose to play it safe and play 1.

Harsanyi and Selten formulate the concept of *risk dominance*, defined later, to capture this idea of the relative riskiness of two strategies. While they argue that Pareto dominance arguments are more forceful than risk dominance arguments in selecting an outcome, the experiment allows us to evaluate which of these two forces is more important in the play of this coordination game. In particular, for this game the risk dominant equilibrium is $\{1, 1\}$ while the payoff dominant equilibrium is clearly $\{2, 2\}$.

In fact, Cooper et al. provide evidence that the outcome is dictated by risk dominance. In their experiment, subjects played $CG - 2 \times 2$ against a sequence of opponents. A cohort was composed of 11 players and each played against the 10 others twice, though not in any observable or predictable order. At no point in the experiment did the players know the identity or the history of play of their opponent. In this sense, the outcomes represent a sequence of one-shot games. Finally, the payoffs indicated in the matrix refer to points players could earn in each period of play. After the actions were simultaneously selected and the outcome determined, a lottery was run in which players received a monetary payoff if and only if (iff) the number of points they earned exceeded the number of the lottery ticket. In this way, differences across players in attitudes toward risk are eliminated since they all will maximize the probability of winning the lottery.

The results reported by Cooper et al. indicate that coordination failures can certainly arise in experimental settings. In other words, the view that the Pareto-dominant outcome acts as a focal point is not supported by observed outcomes. For the last 11 periods of play of Game CG, Cooper et al. find that 97% of the play occurs at the {1, 1} equilibrium. There are no observations of the {2, 2} equilibrium. Thus risk dominance provides a better guide in this game than does Pareto dominance.

Other experimental coordination games are described in van Huyck, Battalio and Beil [1990] and Cooper et al. [1990]. Van Huyck et al. examine a finitely repeated coordination game. Following the coordination model of Bryant [1983], a structure we consider in the following chapter, the payoffs of each player are given by

$$\pi(e_i, e_{-i}) = a[\min(e_i, e_{-i})] - be_i \tag{1}$$

In these payoffs, e_i is the choice of agent i and e_{-i} is the vector of choices by the other players. In their experiment, van Huyck et al. restrict the strategy space of each agent to the set of integers between 1 and 7. Assuming that $a > b > 0$, there are multiple Pareto-ranked Nash equilibria for this coordination game. In particular, any strategy profile with $e_i = e$ for all i and $e \in \{1, 2, 3, 4, 5, 6, 7\}$ is an equilibrium of the stage game with the equilibrium in which all $e_i = 7$ for all i Pareto dominating the others.

Note that this game differs from those we have considered so far in that dynamics are present through the play of finite repetitions of the stage game. The set of equilibria for this finitely repeated coordination game includes all of the Nash equilibria from the one-shot game. In fact, repeating this coordination game does not expand the set of equilibrium outcomes.

However, the repetitions do allow for learning about the actions of others and thus the resolution of strategic uncertainty.

In their basic treatment, van Huyck et al. choose $a = \$0.2$ and $b = \$0.1$ to parameterize the payoff functions. These payoffs were presented to the subjects through a payoff table rather than through any functional relationship. There were between 14 and 16 subjects involved in these treatments and play was repeated 10 times. After each period of play, subjects were told the minimum of the actions selected by others in that period of play. No other information about other players, such as which one chose the minimum, was disclosed.

One important finding by van Huyck et al. is that the Pareto-dominant Nash equilibrium is not observed. While there is some play of action 7 in early periods, these choices quickly disappear as players recognize that others are choosing lower actions. In fact, over time play tends to converge to the Nash equilibrium with the lowest effort level, $e_i = 1$ for all i. Interestingly enough, this outcome is the same as that which would occur if all players chose their maximum action. That is, action 1 is the choice that maximizes the payoffs of a player given that he believes others will select an action that minimizes that player's payoffs. The outcome $e_i = 1$ for all i is thus termed the "secure outcome."

Van Huyck et al. [1990] consider a number of variations of this basic treatment. First, they alter the game by setting $b = 0$ so that effort is costless. In this case, there is a dominant strategy, which is $e_i = 7$ for all i. After 15 periods, play converged to the dominant strategy equilibrium though there is play of dominated strategies in earlier rounds.

A second variation concerned reducing the number of players. One might argue that reducing the number of players would reduce the probability of at least one player's choosing the lowest action and thus make the secure equilibrium less likely. When two players were paired to play the coordination game with $a = \$0.20$ and $b = \$0.10$, play converged to the Pareto-dominant Nash equilibrium for 12 out of 14 pairs of players. This contrasts with the results for two-player games reported by Cooper et al. [1992], though, of course, there are important differences in the payoff matrices.

Coordination failures in yet another experimental environment are described by Cooper et al. [1990]. In this experiment, there is a sequence of one-shot games using the same design as in Cooper et al. [1992]. However, instead of a 2×2 coordination game, they study a symmetric 3×3 game in which strategy 3 supports the joint payoff maximum, given in Figure 1.2 as CG $- 3 \times 3$. The variables x and y were varied across

Player *B*

		1	2	3
Player *A*	1	350, 350	350, 250	$x, 0$
	2	250, 350	550, 550	$y, 0$
	3	$0, x$	$0, y$	600, 600

CG -3×3

Figure 1.2

treatments with the intent of understanding how variations in these parameters influenced the equilibrium selection. In particular, consider two leading cases: Case 1, in which $(x, y) = (1000, 0)$, and Case 2, in which $(x, y) = (700, 1000)$. Note that for both of these parameterizations, strategy 3 is dominated. In Case 1, strategy 1 dominates 3, and in Case 2, strategy 3 is dominated by both strategies 1 and 2. Yet, as in the prisoner's dilemma game, strategy 3 supports the joint payoff maximum in both cases. Thus this game combines a coordination game with a prisoner's dilemma.

Cooper et al. find that for all of the parameterizations, play is predominantly at one of the pure strategy Nash equilibria. For Case 1, the Pareto-inferior Nash equilibrium is observed, while the Pareto-dominant Nash equilibrium is played in Case 2. Interestingly enough, the equilibrium selected in a given treatment depended on the returns to playing strategy 3, a dominated strategy. That is, the best response to strategy 3 is 1 in Case 1 and 2 in Case 2. In this way, tracing the best response to the play of the cooperative, though dominated, strategy leads to the selection of the equilibrium outcome. This is further supported by the fact that in early periods of the treatment, there is considerable play of the cooperative strategy, as in experimental prisoner's dilemma games. However, Cooper et al. do find that for a third case, $(x, y) = (700, 650)$, play eventually evolves to the (2, 2) outcome even though the best response to 3 is strategy 1.

While no single explanation appears fully consistent with the observations, it should be noted that this game is quite complex in that it incorporates both the desires to cooperate and the concerns over strategic uncertainty noted earlier. From that perspective, it is quite surprising that play did in fact evolve to one of the Nash equilibria! Overall, this experiment provides further evidence of the possibility of coordination failures and points to the fact that variations in payoffs associated with an opponent's play of a dominated strategy can influence equilibrium outcomes.

In addition to providing examples of coordination failures, these experimental exercises have provided insights into conditions under which variations in the game may prevent these outcomes. Two such variations are particularly relevant: preplay communication and the importance of outside options.

Preplay Communication

Suppose that, prior to the play of a coordination game, the row player sends a message to the column player. Instead of allowing any form of communication, suppose that the message in this communication stage is constrained to be an element of row's strategy space. Further, suppose that this message does not bind row's choice in the next stage of the game. These are often called games with *cheap talk* since the messages are costless to send and nonbinding.

Given this two-stage game, a number of important questions emerge. What message should row send? How should the column player respond to row's message? Surely there are equilibria in which the actions chosen correspond to those selected in the one-stage coordination game so that row's announcements have no influence on play. Interestingly enough, there may be other equilibria in which cheap talk can matter.

Farrell [1987] argued that there is another, reasonable equilibrium, in which announcements are taken at face value if (i) it will indeed be optimal for the sender to keep his promise and (ii) he expects the receiver to believe the message. In this fashion, one-way cheap talk permits row to select the Nash equilibrium of his choice. For the coordination game denoted as $CG - 2 \times 2$ earlier, the predicted outcome is $(2, 2)$ as row effectively chooses the equilibrium that will be played in the second stage of the game. In this way, all coordination problems are resolved.

If communication is permitted in both directions, the story is slightly more complicated. Again following Farrell [1987], assume the following:

  a. If the announcements of both players constitute a pure-strategy Nash equilibrium for the second-stage game, each player will play his announced strategy, and
  b. If the announcements of both players do not constitute a pure-strategy equilibrium in the second-stage game, each player will behave as if the communication had never happened and play strategy 1.

With these assumptions, two-way preplay communication will, at least in theory, resolve coordination problems in $CG - 2 \times 2$. Given the response to the combinations of announcements given earlier, announcing 2 is a dominant strategy. To see this, note that if one player announces 2, the other player should do so as well to guarantee the Pareto-dominant outcome, which gives the highest payoffs to each of the two players. Further, if one player announces 1, then the other cannot do any worse by announcing 2.

Cooper et al. [1992] find that preplay communication is quite effective in overcoming coordination problems when both players send announcements. Under this two-way communication treatment, over 90% of the outcomes during the last 11 periods of play were at the {2, 2} outcome. Further, all of the announcements in the last 11 periods were of strategy 2.

For one-way communication, the effect of cheap talk was not nearly as strong. Cooper et al. find that the Pareto-dominant equilibrium is achieved about 53% of the time, but this falls far short of the outcome achieved through two-way communication. In the one-way communication treatment, the row player announces strategy 2 about 87% of the time but does not always follow through on this suggestion, nor does column follow with the play of 2.

One interpretation of these results corresponds to the idea that risk dominance is the resource of the coordination problem. That is, given the riskiness of playing strategy 2 in the coordination game, players need sufficient confidence that the other will select this strategy as well. As a consequence, the announcement of one player is simply not strong enough to overcome the riskiness of strategy 2. It appears that both players must announce 2 in order to support the Pareto-dominant outcome.

Outside Options and Forward Induction

A second variation on the basic coordination game is to allow one player the option of receiving a sure outcome instead of playing the coordination game. This creates another two-stage game in which the power of *forward induction*, as described in Kohlberg and Mertens [1986], can be explored.

Suppose that the outside option is sufficiently high that it dominates the payoffs from one of the strategies in the coordination game. In this case, if row elects to play the game, then column should believe that row will not play the strategy dominated by the outside option. Thus, if the outside option in $CG - 2 \times 2$ exceeds 800, then by the logic of forward induction, row should reject the outside option and both row and column should select strategy 2 in the coordination game.

Cooper et al. [1992] report that when the coordination game, CG – 2 × 2, was played with a prior stage in which row had the choice of a "relevant" outside option paying 900, play changed rather dramatically. Conditional on row's rejecting the outside option and selecting the subgame, 77% of outcomes were at the Pareto-dominant equilibrium and only 2% at (1, 1). These are consistent with forward induction. Contrary to the predictions of forward induction, however, the outside option was selected almost 40% of the time.

Van Huyck et al. [1993] report results concerning the introduction of an auction in which the rights to play a coordination game are traded so that, through forward-induction-type arguments, the auction coordinates outcomes. That is, consider a multiple-player coordination game, in which the payoffs are given by

$$\pi(e_i, M) = aM - b(M - e_i)^2 \tag{2}$$

where M is the median action chosen by the N (odd) players and $e_i \in \{1, 2, \dots E\}$ where E is the largest feasible integer value. This is a coordination game in which there are multiple, Pareto-ranked equilibria since the best response of each player is to choose an action equal to the median action as long as $b > 0$.

Prior to playing this game, suppose that an auction is held in which more than N players participate in bidding for the right to play the coordination game. The equilibrium value associated with the auction ought, according to the forward-induction logic, also influence play of the subsequent coordination game. Players who intend to select "low effort" strategies should not be willing to pay a very high price for playing the game. Put differently, a high entry fee signals that players will not select strategies that will lead them to be worse off than having not paid to participate in the game at all.

Using a parameterization of $a = \$0.1$ and $b = \$0.05$, van Huyck et al. [1993] find that when the coordination game is played by nine subjects for 10 periods without a first-stage auction, the outcome was never the payoff-dominant equilibrium. As in the similar games reported in van Huyck et al. [1991], coordination failures were observed.

The most interesting part of the experiment concerns the effects of adding an auction stage prior to the play of the coordination game. In the auction stage, 18 subjects bid for the right to be one of the 9 players participating in the coordination game. Van Huyck et al. employed an English Clock auction, in which initially the price is set low so that all subjects indicate they are willing to buy the asset. At a fixed time interval, the price is increased by a fixed amount. As the price is increased, subjects "exit" by indicating that they are unwilling to pay the posted price for a seat in the coordination game. Once there are only 9 players remaining in the auction, the auction stops and those players are selected for the coordination game.

In their two-stage treatments, the auction stage was followed by the play of the above coordination game in each period. This two-stage game was repeated either 10 or 15 times with the same group of subjects. Van Huyck et al. report that the price in the auction and the actions taken in the coordination game were not independent. Most strikingly, play converged to the payoff-dominant Nash equilibrium, and the price of a seat in the game was bid up to the payoff from this equilibrium of the coordination game. In this sense, the auction served to coordinate activity.

Learning and Dynamics

One of the fascinating aspects of experimental games is the time series of play. Yet, for the most part, the analysis of experimental data stresses the outcomes observed over the last few periods of play. This is unfortunate given the richness of play that underlies the "convergence" process.

For coordination games, the time series of play has begun to receive attention. As we have noted already, the multiplicity of equilibria in these games implies that agents face uncertainty (often termed *strategic uncertainty*) over the actions of others. Thus, it is likely that the selection of an equilibrium can be traced to the time path of play in an experimental coordination game since agents may all be using the past to predict the future behavior of others. Put differently, history matters in these games and uncovering the influence of the past on the selection of an equilibrium is important.

A useful starting point for this discussion is the analysis of the coordination games in Crawford [1991, 1995]. This paper lays out a specification for behavior in these games and provides explicit links to the evidence provided in van Huyck et al. [1990, 1991].

In the dynamic game, there are $i = 1, \dots, I$ players involved in a repeated game. The basic model of behavior describes player i's action in period t (x_{it}) as

$$x_{it} = \alpha_i + \beta_t y_{t-1} + (1 - \beta_t)x_{it-1} + \varepsilon_{it} \tag{3}$$

where y_{t-1} is a summary statistic from play in period t. In this specification, the parameters describing the behavior of the agents (α_t, β_t) evolve over time and are reflected in differences in the weights placed on the two elements of past behavior. Finally, there are individual shocks allowed in the specification so that "errors" are part of the model.

Crawford notes that this decision rule cannot be rationalized from optimizing behavior. Instead, it is productive to think of it as a specification of a decision rule that may capture some important aspects of the data: principally the feedback from past aggregate (y_{t-1}) and individual decisions (x_{it-1}) on current ones.

Crawford explores a version of this model, with actions in a discrete set, to understand the observations generated by van Huyck et al. [1990, 1991]. For this empirical work, α_t and β_t were allowed to vary over time and the variance of the "decision error" ε_{it} was assumed to fall over time at a fixed rate (λ). Thus the key parameters to estimate were α, β and λ along with the variances of the shocks.

Crawford estimates this model using the panel data provided from a variety of the van Huyck experiments. The interested reader should consult Crawford [1995] for a detailed discussion of the empirical approach and fit.

Overall, the model does quite well in the versions of experimental games where payoffs depend on the *median* efforts of others, as in (2), where play tended to converge to the median play observed in the initial round. So, for some of the treatments, the estimate of β is quite close to 1. Further, Crawford finds evidence of the dispersion in individual behavior needed to sustain the theme that strategic uncertainty is an important aspect of these games. The model does less well in terms of the mean effort games, such as (1). In particular, in contrast to the median game, the estimated variances of the shocks to behavior did not appear to fall over time.

EQUILIBRIUM SELECTION

This experimental evidence seems quite convincing in terms of dispelling the view that coordination problems will not occur in simple strategic interactions. Complementary to the accumulation of evidence on coordination games has been the development of theories concerning equilibrium selection in these games. We turn to some of those theories now.

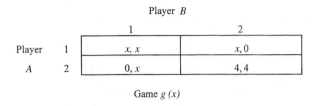

Game $g\,(x)$

Figure 1.3

Risk Dominance

As argued by Harsanyi and Selten, one basis for selection is risk dominance. The point of this concept is to make precise the intuition that playing certain equilibrium strategies is riskier than playing others given the underlying strategic uncertainty of a game. Of course, risky strategies may support the Pareto-dominant equilibrium. If so, a tradeoff emerges between risk and return.

To define and illustrate this concept we use the following game, borrowed from Carlsson and van Damme [1993] and labeled Game $g(x)$ in Figure 1.3. The set of equilibria will depend on the value of x. For $x < 0$, the equilibrium in which each player chooses strategy 2 is a dominant strategy equilibrium. Similarly, when $x > 4$, strategy 1 is dominant for both players. The coordination problems arise when $x\ \varepsilon\ (0, 4)$. In this case there are multiple pure-strategy equilibria. Note that these equilibria are Pareto-ordered. Following Carlsson and van Damme, let $V(s)$ be the net gain for a player from choosing action 1 rather than action 2 when the other player is choosing action 1 with probability s. For this example, $V(s) = x - (1 - s)4$. Let s^* solve $V(s) = 0$ so that $s^* = (4 - x)/4$ in this example. So if a player attaches probability less than or equal to s^* that his opponent will choose action 1, then that player ought to select action 2. Likewise, if the probability associated with an opponent's choice of 1 exceeds s^*, then action 1 should be chosen. So a low value of s^* implies a wider range of beliefs that would justify the choice of action 1.

This observation is the critical link to the concept of risk dominance. Suppose that agents enter into this strategic interaction with uniform priors about the likely action of their opponent. The uniformity of priors implies that they expect to face an opponent who selects strategy 1 with probability .5. By symmetry, the other player thinks the same. So, if $s^* < .5$, then each player, given these beliefs, should choose action 1 and the equilibrium in which both players select 1 is said to be risk dominant. This occurs in Game $g(x)$ whenever $x > 2$. In this case, we see that risk dominance may yield a different prediction than payoff dominance.

For the game labeled CG – 2 × 2 in Figure 1.1, $V(s) = 800 - (1 - s)1000$ so that $s^* = .2$. Therefore the equilibrium in which players select strategy 1 is risk dominant. Note that in the 3 × 3 coordination game illustrated in Figure 1.2, after deletion of the dominated strategy, the risk dominant equilibrium is (2, 2) since $s^* = 2/3$. Since this value of s^* is independent of the treatment variables (x, y), risk dominance alone is not sufficient to explain the results of that experiment. Further, as discussed by Crawford [1995], risk dominance does not accurately predict the outcome of the van Huyck et al. [1990] experiments.

Games of Incomplete Information

In an ingenious paper, Carlsson and van Damme provide an argument for selection of an equilibrium from a coordination game. Their idea is to explore the equilibria of a nearby game of incomplete information. The equilibrium for the coordination game is then the limit of the equilibrium for the nearby game as the amount of incomplete information goes to zero. In fact, they find that in the limit it is the risk-dominant equilibrium that is selected.

Carlsson and van Damme study risk dominance through their creation of a game of incomplete information that is close to Game $g(x)$. In particular, suppose that x is a random variable uniformly distributed on $[x^-, x^+]$ with [0, 4] lying inside this interval. Thus, the domain of x includes realizations of $g(x)$ in which there are multiple equilibria as well as realizations with dominant strategy equilibria. The incomplete information arises because players do not observe x. Rather, player i observes a signal, s^i, which, Carlsson and van Damme assume, is uniformly distributed on $[x - \varepsilon, x + \varepsilon]$. Thus the magnitude of ε determines the informativeness of the signal. Note that the signal is informative about both the underlying state (x) and the signal of the other player, s^{-i}, since the signals are correlated with x. Once agents receive their signals, they are involved in a game of incomplete information: they do not know exactly what payoff they will receive as a function of the action they select.

Given this structure, one can informally see how the incomplete information "resolves" the coordination problem.[2] The idea is that the dominant strategy aspect of the game when $x < 0$ and $x > 4$ will spill over to generate a unique outcome when x is between 0 and 4 and the signal is very informative. The point is that players conceive of the possibility that their opponent has received a signal such that one or the other strategy is dominant, thus pinning down the play. This is true for extreme signals and, through the construction of the equilibrium, true for less extreme signals as well.

To see this a bit more formally, suppose that ε is less than $-x^-/2$ and player i observes $s^i < 0$. As the signal is within ε of the true value of x and $x^- < 0$, player i's view must be that x is negative. In particular, note that the conditional expectation of x given s^i is s^i. Hence, the payoff to action 1 is negative and thus selecting 2 is a dominant strategy.

Given this, what if player i observers $s^i = 0$? Then player i realizes that with probability .5 the other player $(-i)$ has a signal that is negative, which, from the previous argument, implies the play of the dominant strategy 2 by player $-i$. With $s^i = 0$, the expected return to playing 1 is 0 and this is less than the expected return from 2 given that player $-i$ will select 2 with probability at least .5. So, action 1 is dominated when player i receives the signal s^i. So, for any $s_i \leq 0$, the play of 2 is a dominant strategy.

What if s_i is slightly bigger than 0? In this case, player i thinks that player $-i$ has received a negative signal with probability close to .5, and thus the probability that $-i$ will play 2 is, at least, very close to .5. Player i, though, recognizes that player $-i$ may have received a positive signal. In that case, what will player $-i$ choose?

To answer this question, we must consider the entire equilibrium: the mapping from signals into actions. Carlsson and van Damme argue that there is a critical value of the signal, call it s^*, such that strategy 2 is a dominant strategy for player i whenever $s_i < s^*$. So, if player i observes the signal s^*, he must assign at least probability .5 that player $-i$ will choose action 2. Therefore, choosing 2 will generate a payoff of at least 2. For 2 not to be a dominant strategy at $s_i = s^*$, it must be the case that the expected payoff from playing 1 is at least 2. Further, since the expected return from 1 is s^*, then $s^* \geq 2$ is necessary for strategy 2 not to be dominant when $s_i = s^*$ is observed.

By a symmetric argument, one can start with signals above 4, in which

2. See Carlsson and van Damme for the formal argument.

case strategy 1 is a dominant strategy. As the signal falls toward 2 from above, there will be a point such that action 1 is no longer a dominant strategy. As in the preceding argument, this critical signal cannot exceed 2; otherwise, the expected return from strategy 1 would be high enough that strategy 2 would be dominated.

Putting these two pieces together, the critical signal for this game is $s^* = 2$. Each player will select action 1 if $s > s^*$ and 2 otherwise. Thus, the players each select the strategy corresponding to the risk-dominant equilibrium of the game, $g(s_i)$!

As noted by Carlsson and van Damme, this does not mean that the equilibrium outcome of the game of incomplete information will always be the risk-dominant equilibrium of the coordination game for the realized value of x since the players' signals may be on opposite sides of s^*. Of course, as ε gets small, the chances this will occur are close to zero. The main point of the Carlsson–van Damme paper is to formalize the intuition from this example.

Learning and Dynamics

Another approach to equilibrium selection involves exploring the dynamics of coordination games. Of course, to do so requires the specification of a dynamic process describing the play of agents involved in such a game. This means that we must go beyond the Nash equilibrium concept since it does not specify a process of equilibrium.

One recent approach rests upon the work of Kandori, Mailath and Rob [1993]. These authors stress three main aspects for their dynamic model: inertia, myopia and mutation. Let's explore these in turn. *Inertia* creates some "stickiness" in the dynamics in that not all agents reoptimize every period. It may be that agents react in a time dependent fashion (i.e., adjusting every few periods) or in a state dependent manner (i.e., adjusting when the state is far enough from a target). The key is that all agents are not reacting immediately to their environment.

Myopia implies that when agents do adjust their actions, they ignore the dynamic consequences of their choices. This is a type of bounded rationality view in that players are assumed to be unable to contemplate the strategic implications of their actions. In many cases, myopia is modeled by assuming that players best respond to the *current* actions of other players.

Mutation is the basis for mistakes and, as we shall see, for movement away from certain pure strategy equilibria of the game. Put differently, the possibility that players' actions are not best responses adds noise to the dynamical system. It is precisely this noise that creates a unique outcome, in the form of a distribution across actions. Further, because of mutation, it is possible to have multiple "defections" from an equilibrium profile of strategies and thus for the agents to "move" away from an equilibrium.

Kandori, Mailath and Rob provide further motivation for these components. Clearly, though, the intent is to move beyond the Nash equilibrium view of forward looking, completely rational agents and to substitute certain behavioral rules that have the desired property of reproducing some of the Nash equilibria at the limits of parameter space. That is, the dynamical system does "select" one of the Nash equilibria as the mutation rate becomes small.

Consider the following example, which is meant to illustrate these three components.[3] There are N (assumed to be even) players involved in a coordination game. In each period, the players are randomly matched and each pair plays a coordination game such as $g(x)$. Once the pairs are set, with probability δ a player can alter his strategy. Otherwise the player is required to choose the same action as in the previous period. This is a simple way to model inertia. Further, if a player can change his strategy, it is assumed that the player best responds to the strategy profile of all players from the period before. Thus the player does not respond in any way to the actions of the player he is currently paired with, nor does the player look forward to anticipate the consequences of this strategy choice. Finally, with probability $(1 - m)$ the action of the player is the one chosen and with probability m the player makes a "mistake." For games with two actions, such as the coordination game under study, a mistake means that the action of the player is the strategy that was not chosen.

So, in a given period, there are $N/2$ pairs that are formed. Let s_t be the strategy profile from period t and p_t represent the fraction of players choosing action 1 in period t. A fraction of the players is permitted to adjust their strategies, and, by assumption, these players best respond to p_t. Further, by mutation, only a fraction $(1 - m)$ play this best response. The remainder end up playing the other strategy. The interaction of inertia, myopia and mutation produces a strategy profile p_{t+1} and the stochastic process continues. Note that the randomness in the profiles reflects both

---

3. This example is a bit more formal than that given in Section 2 of their paper.

the probabilistic nature of the adjustment process (each agent can change his strategy with probability δ) and the mutation process (*m*).

Intuitively, the equilibrium selection process reflects both (δ, *m*). If δ = 1 and *m* = 0, then players can adjust their strategy each period and do so without making any mistakes. In this case, we are back to the multiple equilibrium model since strategy profiles at either of the pure strategy Nash equilibria will be steady states of this system. In particular, recall that agents best respond to the profile in the previous period so that there will never be any movement away from a pure strategy equilibrium. If the strategy profile is not one of the pure strategy equilibria, then players will best respond and in a single period drive the system to one of the pure strategy equilibria.[4]

Here there is an issue of selection that reduces to knowing the basins of attraction for the pure strategy equilibria. For the game $g(x)$, if p_t exceeds s^*, then players will best respond by selecting strategy 1, leading to the {1, 1} equilibrium. Else, if p_t is strictly less than s^*, then the {2, 2} outcome will be observed. Note the important role that is again played by s^*, the probability such that a player is indifferent between the two actions of game $g(x)$.

Once we no longer restrict δ = 1 and *m* = 0, then inertia and mutation will play a role in the analysis. In particular, δ < 1 and *m* > 0 will slow the dynamics and add noise to the process. The role of noise is most easily understood by considering an example.

Assume that $x = 3$ in Game $g(x)$ so that the {1, 1} equilibrium is risk dominant. As suggested by Kandori, Mailath and Rob there is a strong sense that the {1, 1} equilibrium is more robust to mutations than the Pareto-superior Nash equilibrium. For any $p_{t-1} \geq s^*$, the best response of those selecting actions in period *t* is to select action 1. Since $s^* < .5$, the basin of attraction for the Pareto-inferior equilibrium is larger than that for the Pareto-superior equilibrium. So, starting from the equilibrium in which all players select action 1, the number of mutations needed to move the state of the system, so that p_{t+1} is less than s^*, is relatively large compared to the number of mutations which would move the system away from the Pareto-superior equilibrium. This is *not* to say that play at the (2, 2) equilibrium would not be observed but rather that it is much less likely to be observed. As in the other selection theories, the key is again the large basin of attraction associated with the risk dominant equilibrium.

---

4. Here we are ignoring the case where the strategy profile mimics the mixed strategy equilibrium.

One could take this relatively simple structure and either analyze it directly or create computer simulations of this process. The point would be to understand the mapping between the key parameters (N, δ, m) and the probability distribution of outcomes. In fact, one could then try to match the implications of the theory with evidence from experiments built upon this same structure.

SUMMARY

The point of this chapter was to introduce the basic theme of coordination games and then to explore some of the theories of selection and some of the experimental evidence. By now, the basic elements of the coordination game should be clear. The key points relate to the multiplicity of Nash equilibria and their Pareto ranking. In coordination games, the key element is confidence rather than conflict.

Overall, the evidence points to the fact that Pareto domination does not provide a natural focal point for coordination games. Put differently, coordination failures can arise in experimental games.

At this stage, it is natural to develop further the theoretical basis of coordination problems. This is done in two main stages. First, the next chapter provides a basic framework of analysis, bringing to light, in a more formal manner, the salient features of coordination games. Second, the remaining chapters trace out a wide variety of examples of coordination problems of interest to macroeconomists.

2   A Framework for Analysis

The goal of the previous chapter was to provide an introduction to coordination games and some evidence on coordination failures. In the end, we find that coordination failures can arise in fairly simple experimental settings. While these experiments are certainly suggestive that coordination problems may arise, they leave open an important question: what are the underlying economic interactions that lead to coordination games?

The answer offered in this chapter takes the form of two abstract frameworks for analysis. The first, drawing upon Cooper and John [1988], stresses the interaction between agents in strategic settings where strategies are simply scalars in a closed interval. This formulation leads to a relatively straightforward equilibrium analysis, including conditions for multiple equilibria and some welfare results. The main point is that coordination games, such as those illustrated in the previous chapter, rest upon an interaction between agents termed *strategic complementarity*. As suggested already, this interaction implies that increased effort by other agents leads the remaining agent to follow suit. Besides becoming the basis for multiple equilibria, the strategic complementarity gives rise to multiplier effects.

The second part of the chapter looks at more general interactions. While almost all current macroeconomic applications of coordination games can be cast in the Cooper–John framework, the more general structure, investigated most recently by Milgrom and Roberts [1990] and Vives [1990], is quite powerful and worthy of study.

18

COOPER–JOHN MODEL

Cooper and John [1988] consider a game which highlights the key theme in this literature: the concept of strategic complementarity. Put in simple words, this condition implies that higher actions by other players provide an incentive for the remaining player to take a higher action as well. Making precise the idea of a "higher action" and understanding the conditions under which responses are monotonically increasing in the choices of others are the central focuses of this class of games.

Formally, assume that agent i, $i = 1, 2, \ldots I$, chooses a strategy e_i in the interval $[0, 1]$. Refer to e_i as the activity level or effort of agent i. The strategy set for each agent is completely ordered so that speaking of higher effort levels is well defined. Here one can think of there being I individual agents or I coalitions of agents in an economy. The point is that these I agents choose their activity levels in a noncooperative fashion.

Let $\sigma(e_i, e_{-i}, \theta_i)$ be the payoff of agent i from action e_i where e_{-i} is the vector of actions of other agents and θ_i, a scalar, parameterizes the payoffs of agent i. Assume that these payoff functions are continuously differentiable, with $\sigma_{11} < 0$ and $\sigma_{13} > 0$.[1] That is, payoffs are strictly concave in e_i and marginal returns to effort increase in θ_i.[2] As we shall see, the critical restrictions on payoffs concern the nature of the cross-partial derivatives, which we leave unspecified for now.

To start the analysis, assume $\theta = \theta_i$. As all players are identical, it is natural to focus on symmetric Nash equilibria in which all agents choose the same action.[3] With this in mind, we denote payoffs when all agents other than i choose action e by $\sigma(e_i, e, \theta)$.[4] Therefore, the set of interior, symmetric Nash equilibria is given by

$$\xi(\theta) = \{e \in [0, 1] \mid \sigma_1(e, e, \theta) = 0\}$$

This describes the set of Nash equilibria since the first-order condition for an agent is satisfied at the same action chosen by all of the other agents. Since $\sigma(\cdot)$ is strictly concave, this first-order condition holds at a maximum.

An alternative means of characterizing the set of Nash equilibria is to look at the reaction curve of an individual agent in this game. Let $\phi(e, \theta)$

---

1. Unless noted otherwise, properties are assumed to hold over the entire domain of these functions.
2. This second property is just an ordering of θ.
3. However, one should keep in mind that symmetric games can have asymmetric equilibria.
4. There is a slight abuse of notation since the second argument of the function is now a scalar rather than a vector.

be the optimal action of a representative player if all others select action e and the state if θ. That is, $\phi(e, \theta)$ is the best response function and satisfies the condition that $\sigma_1(\phi(e, \theta), e, \theta) = 0$. Clearly, the set of Nash equilibria, $\xi(\theta)$, is identical to

$$\{e \in [0, 1] \,|\, \phi(e, \theta) = e\}$$

Assume that $\sigma_1(0, 0, \theta) > 0$ and $\sigma_1(1, 1, \theta) < 0$ for all θ implying $\phi(0, \theta) > 0$ and $\phi(1, \theta) < 1$. That is, if all other agents chose effort levels at one extreme or the other, the remaining agent has an incentive to choose an effort level which is interior (relative to the choice of others). As $\sigma(\cdot)$ is continuous by assumption, these conditions imply the existence of at least one interior equilibrium. If these boundary conditions on σ_1 were not imposed, then an equilibrium at the extreme of the strategy set will exist. Whether or not there are multiple, symmetric Nash equilibria will depend upon the reaction of a player to variations in the choice of others, i.e., in the sign and magnitude of σ_{12}.

When $\sigma_{12} > 0$ throughout the entire domain of the function, the game exhibits *strategic complementarity* and if $\sigma_{12} < 0$, then the game exhibits *strategic substitutability*.[5] Under strategic complementarity, the best response of one agent to an increase in the activity of all others is to increase e_i. That is, reaction curves are upward sloping: $\phi(e, \theta)$ is increasing in e. As we shall see, this strategic complementarity condition is necessary for the existence of multiple symmetric Nash equilibria and is key to the propagation of shocks across agents and across time. When strategy spaces are convex and payoff functions are continuously differentiable, the assumption of strategic complementarity is equivalent to the condition of *increasing first differences,* a concept described by Milgrom–Roberts and Vives and used in the following section.

Figure 2.1 illustrates a reaction curve that satisfies strategic complementarity in which there exist multiple equilibria, e_l, e_m and e_h. Note too that these equilibria change only slightly with variations in θ. In particular, except for very special cases, the number of equilibria is locally constant. This is what we meant earlier by the assertion that the set of equilibria was stable under small perturbations of the game.

The following propositions are from Cooper and John [1988]. They

---

5. At this point we have restricted attention to symmetric outcomes and hence to $e_j = e$ for all $j \neq i$. Hence we require these cross-derivative properties for this restricted part of the strategy space. Unless specified otherwise, think of these as global properties: i.e., conditions that hold over the entire domain.

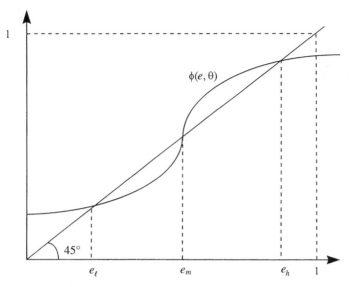

Figure 2.1

provide a relationship between strategic complementarity and the multiplicity of symmetric Nash equilibria, a welfare ordering of the equilibria and a characterization of multipliers in this environment.

Proposition 1 (Cooper–John [1988]): *If the game exhibits strategic substitutability globally, then there is a unique symmetric Nash equilibrium.*

Proof: Suppose, to the contrary, that there exist two symmetric Nash equilibria, $e_l < e_h$. By definition of symmetric Nash equilibria, $e_l = \phi(e_l, \theta)$ and $e_h = \phi(e_h, \theta)$. The existence of strategic substitutes implies that $\phi(e_l, \theta) > \phi(e_h, \theta)$ since $e_l < e_h$. This is in contradiction to the statement that e_l and e_h are both Nash equilibria with $e_l < e_h$.

QED.

Intuitively, the proposition makes the simple point that the graph of a downward sloping reaction curve will cross the 45-degree line once. Clearly, strategic complementarity, an upward sloping reaction curve, is necessary for multiple equilibria. However, even a positive slope is not sufficient: the slope must exceed 1 at an equilibrium point for there to be multiple crossings, as located in Figure 2.1. That is, a sufficient condition for multiple symmetric Nash equilibria is that $\phi_1(e, \theta) > 1$ for some e in

$\xi(\theta)$. So, for example, if reaction curves have a slope that is always less than 1, then an economy with strategic complementarity will not have multiple Nash equilibria. The example economies that we turn to in the following chapters provide cases in which the strategic complementarity is sufficiently strong that multiple symmetric Nash equilibria result.

To understand the welfare implications in these models, assume that $\sigma_2(\cdot) > 0$. That is, increased effort by all other agents increases the payoffs of the remaining agent so that *positive spillovers* are present.

> **Proposition 2 (Cooper–John [1988]):** *If there are multiple symmetric Nash equilibria and the game exhibits positive spillovers, then the equilibria are Pareto-ordered by the level of activity, e.*

> **Proof:** Let $W(e, \theta)$ be the payoff to an agent if all agents select action e in state θ: i.e., $W(e, \theta) = \sigma(\phi(e, \theta), e, \theta)$. Let e_l and e_h be elements of ζ with $e_l < e_h$.

$$W(e_h, \theta) - W(e_l, \theta) = \int_{e_l}^{e_h} W_1(e, \theta)de \int_{e_l}^{e_h} \sigma_2(\phi(e, \theta), e, \theta)de > 0$$

> By our assumption of positive spillovers, this last term is positive. Note that here we integrate along the best response function and thus use the fact that $\sigma_1(\phi(e, \theta), e, \theta) = 0$.   QED.

This result is important in thinking about the welfare implications of economies with spillovers and strategic complementarity. Figure 2.2 illustrates the payoff functions of a single agent for the two equilibrium levels of effort. The presence of positive spillovers implies that the function in which all other agents choose e_l lies below the function in which they all select e_h.

From this proposition, we see that the economy can become stuck at a Pareto-inferior Nash equilibrium. That is, *coordination failures* can arise in this environment. Further, given the assumption of positive spillovers, the Pareto-inferior Nash equilibria are associated with low economic activity.

In addition to leading to the possibility of multiple, Pareto-ranked equilibria, strategic complementarity has implications for the propagation of shocks. Consider first the impact on the economy of a change in θ, i.e., a common shock. Assume that the economy has a unique equilibrium. The economy is said to have a *multiplier* if the equilibrium response of

selection. That is, if one starts at one of the equilibria and the parameter θ changes, which element in the new set of equilibria will be the outcome? In the absence of a selection criterion, no precise prediction can be made. As we shall discuss in the next section of this chapter, fairly general statements can be made about movements in the set of equilibria as a parameter changes.

Returning to the themes of this chapter, this model gives us some immediate insights into the potential role of coordination games for macroeconomics. In the event that the strategic complementarity gives rise to multiple equilibria, the presence of positive spillovers will lead to a welfare ordering of the Nash equilibria. This gives a specific structure for understanding how individual economies might become stuck in a Pareto-inferior equilibrium with low levels of economic activity. Of course, a convincing argument along these lines requires the discussion of macroeconomic contexts which can be represented by a coordination game. That is the goal of the next chapters. Before pursuing that theme, we continue the presentation of coordination games by turning to a discussion of supermodular games. In addition to discussing these games, the next section also presents the results of simple learning rules and the process of iterative deletion applied to coordination games.

SUPERMODULAR GAMES

In this part of the chapter, we study a general class of games called *supermodular games*. The previous discussion from Cooper and John as well as many macroeconomic coordination games fall into this more general class. There were two key elements in the games discussed: the ability to order elements in the strategy space of the players and the assumption of strategic complementarity that implied upward sloping reaction curves. Here we consider a more general class of games that place related restrictions on strategy spaces and payoff functions and lead to quite close conclusions regarding the nature of best responses and the set of equilibria.

Definitions and Notation

We consider a class of games termed *supermodular games* by Topkis [1978, 1979] and studied more recently by Vives [1985, 1990] and Milgrom and Roberts [1990].[6] These games differ from more general noncooperative games in that the restrictions on strategy spaces and payoffs give rise to positive feedback effects: as other players select higher strategies, the remaining player will as well. The basic characteristics of supermodular games will give rise to ordered strategy sets and monotone best responses that underlie this theme of positive feedback.

As in the previous subsection, consider a game between players indexed $i = 1, 2, \ldots I$. Each player has a strategy set $S_i \subset \mathbb{R}^m$ and selects a strategy $s_i \in S_i$. Let $s \equiv (s_1 \ldots \ldots \ldots s_i) \in S$ denote a strategy combination or profile, where S is the set of joint strategies and is a subset of $\mathbb{R}^{lm}$. Further, let $s_{-i} = (s_1, \ldots s_{i-1}, s_{i+1}, \ldots \ldots s_i) \in S_{-i}$ denote the vector of strategies by players other than i. Finally, the payoff to player i is given by $\sigma_i(s_i, s_{-i}) \in \mathbb{R}$.

Each player takes the action of the others as given and selects a strategy that maximizes his payoff. Let $br_i(s_i) \subset S_i$ denote the best response correspondence for player i given the actions of others, $s_{-i} \in S_{-i}$. That is, $x \in br_i(s_{-i})$ implies that $\sigma_i(x, s_{-i}) \geq \sigma_i(s_i', s_{-i})$ for all $s_i' \in S_i$.

Using these concepts, we first define and then explain the three basic components of supermodular games. A game is a *supermodular game* if, for each i,

1. S_i is a *complete lattice*
2. σ_i exhibits *increasing first differences* in s_i and s_{-i}
3. σ_i is *supermodular* in s_i (given s_{-i})

As was noted in our discussion of the simple bimatrix coordination game, the gains to a higher action by one player increase with the strategy taken by the other. For the coordination game given in the previous section, the best response function was monotone in the common strategy of the other players, as indicated in Figure 2.1. To formalize this idea for more general games requires some restrictions on the strategy space so that it is natural to talk of higher actions; this is the role of restricting the strategy space to be a complete lattice. Further, best responses must have a monotone structure. When strategies are simply scalars, instead of vectors, the second property of supermodular games is all that is needed to ensure monotone best responses. When actions are vectors, we need an additional restriction to guarantee that all components of a player's best

---

6. To be more precise, Topkis [1978, 1979] analyzed submodular games in which players acted to minimize costs while Vives and Milgrom and Roberts consider supermodular games in which payoff maximization is the objective.

response vector move together. That, as we shall see, is the main role of the third property.

The first restriction in this definition is that the strategy space is a complete lattice. In the convectional analysis of Nash equilibrium, the strategy set of each player is often assumed to be compact and convex. That structure is not required in the analysis of supermodular games. Instead, S_i is restricted to be a complete lattice; that restriction, as described later, implies that it is possible to partially order the feasible strategies. This ordering of strategies, combined with the restrictions on payoffs, substitutes for the conventional convexity restrictions to generate best response correspondences which are "well-behaved" enough to obtain a fixed point. To understand the meaning of the restriction placed on the strategy sets, we define the concept of a lattice as well as the closely related concepts of a complete lattice and a sublattice.

A *lattice* is a partially ordered set in which any two elements have a greatest lower bound (inf) and a least upper bound (sup) in the set.[7] Thus, a lattice requires the specification of a set, say L, and an ordering on that set, denoted by $\leq$, such that the greatest lower and least upper bounds of any two elements of the set exist in the set.

Given a set L, a partial order $\leq$ and $x, y \in L$, then $z \in L$ is the greatest lower bound of x and y in L if $z \leq x$, $z \leq y$, and for all $q \in L$ such that $q \leq x$ and $q \leq y$, it is the case that $q \leq z$. The least upper bound of two points is defined in an analogous way. The least upper bound of (x, y) is often denoted by $x \vee y$ and termed the *join* of x and y. Similarly, the greatest lower bound of (x, y) is often denoted by $x \wedge y$ and termed the *meet* of x and y.

The open interval $(0, 1)$ is a lattice since it is ordered and any two points in the interval have a meet and a join in that interval. The nonconvex set $(0, \frac{1}{2}) \cup (\frac{3}{4}, 1)$ is also a lattice. However, the set $\{(0, 1), (1, 0)\}$ is not a lattice since these two points do not have either a least upper bound or a greatest lower bound in the set under the product order.[8] However, adding the points $(0, 0)$ and $(2, 2)$ to this set creates a lattice since the inf and sup of any pairs of elements are now in the set. To see this, consider again the two elements $(0, 1)$ and $(1, 0)$ of the larger set $\{(0, 0), (0, 1), (1, 0), (2, 2)\}$. The inf, in the set, of these two elements exists and is $(0, 0)$; the

---

7. Vives and Milgrom and Roberts provide relatively condensed mathematical summaries of these concepts.
8. The product order is a partial order in which $x \leq y$ iff $x_i \leq y_i$ for each component i of the vectors. Thus the two elements $(0, 1)$ and $(1, 0)$ do not have either an inf or a sup in the set.

sup in the set also exists and is (2, 2). A frequently used example of a lattice, which is not composed of discrete points, is the set created as the product of n compact subsets of the real line under the product order.

There are two related concepts which are important as well. First, a lattice L is a *complete* lattice if all nonempty subsets of L, say $S \subset L$, have an infimum and a supremum in L: i.e., $\inf_L(S) \in L$ and $\sup_L(S) \in L$. The interval (0, 1) is a lattice but is not complete since the subset (.5, 1) has no least upper bound in (0, 1). In contrast, the lattice [0, 1] is complete since any subset of this set has an inf and a sup in the interval.

Second, a subset of a lattice, $S \subset L$, is a *sublattice* if for $x \in S$ and $y \in S$, the sup(x, y) and the inf(x, y) in L both belong to S. In other words, a sublattice is closed under the meet and join operators.

For example, consider the set $H = \{(0, 0), (1, 0), (0, 1), (1, 1), (2, 1), (1, 2), (2, 2)\}$. H is a lattice under the product order since H is partially ordered and any two elements in the set have an inf and a sup in H. The set $S = \{(0, 0), (1, 0), (0, 1), (1, 1)\}$ is a sublattice of H since the inf and sup, *in the set H*, of any two points in S are elements of S. In contrast, $S' = \{(0, 0), (1, 0), (0, 1), (2, 2)\}$ is also a subset of H but is not a sublattice of H since the join of (1, 0) and (0, 1) in H is (1, 1) and this is not in S'. Note, though, that S' is itself a lattice since (2, 2) is the sup of (1, 0) and (0, 1) in the set S'.

The second part of the definition of supermodular games relates to the interactions across players. In general, if $x, x' \in X$ and $y \in Y$, then $f(x, y)$ exhibits increasing first differences if, for $x \geq x'$, $f(x, y) - f(x', y)$ is (weakly) increasing in y.[9] In a supermodular game, y represents the vector of strategies by other agents and x and x' are strategies of agent i. So, requiring that $\sigma_i(s_i, s_{-i})$ exhibits increasing first differences implies that when all other agents choose higher actions, the gain to player i from selecting a higher action increases: i.e., $\sigma_i(s_i, s_{-i}) - \sigma_i(s'_i, s_{-i})$ is increasing in s_{-i} when $s_i \geq s'_i$. If best responses were unique and payoff functions had increasing first differences, then the best response function would be monotonically increasing in the actions of other players. Thus this part of the definition of a supermodular game captures the restriction on monotone best responses used in the Cooper–John model.

As for the third part of the definition of a supermodular game, a real-valued function $f:L \to \mathbb{R}$ is supermodular if for $x, y \in L$,

---

9. If for $x > x'$, $f(x, y) - f(x', y)$ is strictly increasing in y, then $f(\cdot)$ exhibits strictly increasing first differences.

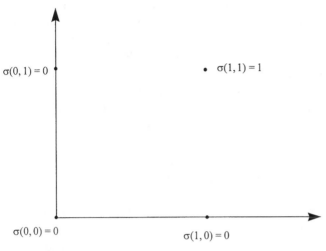

$\sigma(0,1) = 0$ $\sigma(1,1) = 1$

$\sigma(0,0) = 0$ $\sigma(1,0) = 0$

Figure 2.4

$$f(x) + f(y) \leq f(x \wedge y) + f(x \vee y)$$

where L is a lattice.[10] In terms of the payoff functions for our game, this condition implies that

$$\sigma_i(s_i, s_{-i}) + \sigma_i(s'_i, s_{-i}) \leq \sigma_i(s_i \vee s'_i, s_{-i}) + \sigma_i(s_i \wedge s'_i, s_{-i})$$

Figure 2.4 illustrates a supermodular function. Here we assume that the choice space of an agent is a subset of R^2 given by the four points of the square where $s = (s_1, s_2)$ is an element of the choice set. Further, suppose that utility simply depends on the action of this single agent. Payoffs are indicated in brackets at each point in the choice set assuming that $\sigma(s) = \min(s_1, s_2)$. The restriction of supermodularity is that the sum of the payoffs from the strategies $(0, 1)$ and $(1, 0)$ must not exceed the sum of the payoffs from the $(1, 1)$ and $(0, 0)$ strategies. In this case, $\sigma(s)$ is clearly supermodular. Note, though, that if $\sigma(s) = \max(s_1, s_2)$, then the payoff function is no longer supermodular. Again, as supermodularity is being imposed as a restriction on the nature of the interaction between elements of a player's strategy choice, it is not necessary to consider explicitly the interactions across players in this example.

In a supermodular game, assuming that the payoff function for player

---

10. When x and y are ordered, the condition holds with equality. When they are not ordered, we have strict supermodularity if the inequality is strict.

i, σ_i, is supermodular in s_i given s_{-i} means there is a complementarity in the elements of player i's choice vector. Given the choice of the other player(s), a single player is better off combining high activity in one dimension of choice with high activity in another. Put differently, consider two feasible strategies for a player and suppose that payoffs from each exceed the payoffs from the inf of the two strategies. Then, the condition of supermodularity implies that the gain from taking the sup of the two strategies relative to the inf is at least as large as the sum of the gain from the two strategies relative to the inf.

In some cases, it is convenient simply to assume that $\sigma_i(s)$ is supermodular in s, where $s \in S$ is a strategy profile and S, recall, is the product of the strategy sets. As noted by Fudenberg and Tirole [1991], if $\sigma_i(s)$ is supermodular in s, then $\sigma_i(s_i, s_{-i})$ is supermodular in s_i and exhibits increasing first differences.

In the event that the payoff function of an agent is continuously differentiable and $S_i \subset \mathbb{R}^m$, Topkis [1978] (see the discussion in Milgrom and Roberts [1990] as well) states that supermodularity holds if and only if the cross-partial of the payoff function with respect to two components of a given agent's strategy vector is positive: i.e., $\partial^2\sigma_i(s_i, s_{-i})/\partial s_{ij}\partial s_{ik} \geq 0$ for $j \neq k$. Further, the condition for increasing first differences is equivalent to $\partial^2\sigma_i(s_i, s_{-i})/\partial s_{ij}\partial s_{mk} \geq 0$ for $i \neq m$, which is a generalization of strategic complementarity.

To understand the conditions for a supermodular game better, consider a two-player game in which both players have identical strategy sets. In particular, let $S_i = \{(0, 0), (0, 1), (1, 0), (1, 1)\}$ for $i = 1, 2$. The strategy set for each player is a complete lattice under the product order. The payoff function for player $i = 1, 2$ is a mapping from $S_1 \times S_2$ to $\mathbb{R}$. In a supermodular game, given the action of the other player, the payoff function must be supermodular in a player's own strategy. Consider, for example, $\sigma_i(s) = \min(s_k^j)$ where s_k^j is the kth element of j's strategy vector for $j = 1, 2$: i.e., payoffs equal the smallest element in the strategy profile. Suppose player 2 chooses strategy $z = (1, 1) \in S_2$ and let $x = (1, 0)$ and $y = (0, 1)$ be elements of S_1. Then $\sigma_1(x, z) = \sigma_1(y, z) = \sigma_1(x \wedge y, z) = 0$ while $\sigma_1(x \vee y, z) = 1$ so that the condition for supermodularity is met. This condition can easily be checked at other points in $S_1 \times S_2$.

The final condition for a supermodular game is that $\sigma_i(s)$ exhibit increasing first differences. Choose $x = (0, 0)$ and $x' = (1, 1)$ and $z = (0, 0)$ and $z' = (1, 1)$ where $x, x' \in S_1$ and $z, z' \in S_2$. Clearly, $x' \geq x$ and $z' \geq z$ so that the primed actions are higher actions. In our example, $\sigma_1(x, z) = \sigma_1(x', z) =$

$\sigma_1(x, z') = 0$ while $\sigma_1(x', z') = 1$ so that the change in payoffs from a higher strategy is higher when player 2 chooses a higher action (z' rather than z) as required by increasing first differences. The reader can check that these conditions are met at other points in the strategy space.

Existence of a Nash Equilibrium in Supermodular Games

The conventional approach to proving the existence of a Nash equilibrium makes use of Kakutani's fixed point theorem by restricting payoffs and strategy spaces so that the best reply correspondence is convex and upper semicontinuous.[11] For supermodular games we do not impose the requirement that the strategy space is convex, so that the best reply correspondence need not be convex either. As a consequence, an alternative approach is used to prove existence which makes use of the monotone nature of the best reply correspondence under the assumption that the payoff functions are supermodular.[12]

The existence proof requires two types of results. The first is a theorem about the nature of individuals' best response to the actions of others. In particular, do there exist optimal choices for a player given the actions of others and how do these optimal choices respond to the actions of others? Second, there is a fixed point theorem to guarantee the consistency of the individual best responses determined in the first result.

Assuming that the game is supermodular, Topkis [1979, Theorem 3.1] proves the existence of a Nash equilibrium using a fixed point theorem of Tarski [1955]. The fixed point theorem is given by

Theorem 1 (Tarski [1955]): *Let*

(i) $Z = \{S, \leq\}$ be a complete lattice,
(ii) f an increasing function from S to S,
(iii) P be the set of all fixpoint of f,

then the set P is not empty and the system $\{P, \leq\}$ is a complete lattice; in particular, the least upper bound of P and the greatest lower bound of P are in P.

---

11. Topkis [1978] discusses the relationship between supermodularity and convexity, emphasizing that both are second-order properties.
12. Here we modify the approach taken by Topkis [1979] to outline the proof of the existence of Nash equilibria for supermodular games. The interested reader should consult Fudenberg and Tirole [1991] for a more complete proof of existence for supermodular games where strategy sets are subsets of Euclidean space. See also Topkis [1978], Vives [1990] and Milgrom and Roberts [1990] for existence results in other versions of supermodular games.

The key to using this theorem is finding a function (f) that maps from the set of strategy profiles into itself whose fixed point will be a Nash equilibrium. Topkis [1979] uses a selection from the best response correspondence which maps from S to itself. Using the properties of best responses of supermodular functions, one can show that this is an increasing selection from this correspondence. This is, of course, the role of the first type of theorem concerning the nature of the individual's choice problem. The existence of a Nash equilibrium for supermodular games then follows as an application of Tarski's theorem.

To see how this argument works, first consider some properties of the best response correspondence, $br_i(s)$. Topkis [1979, Theorem 1.2] establishes that the set of optimal solutions to the minimization of a submodular, upper semicontinuous function over a compact sublattice is nonempty and contains both a least and a greatest element. Further, these greatest and least elements are monotonically related to a variable (in our case, this will be the strategy profile of other players) which parameterizes payoffs.

Formally, Topkis considers the problem of choosing x to minimize $f(x, y)$ subject to $x \in L \subseteq \mathbb{R}^n$, where L is a lattice, $\mathbb{R}^n$ is n-dimensional Euclidean space and $y \in Y \subseteq \mathbb{R}^m$. Let $L^*(y)$ be the set of optimal solutions to this problem, for a given value of y. Topkis proves that if $f(x, y)$ is upper semicontinuous then (i) $L^*(y)$ is a nonempty compact sublattice with a greatest (least) element and (ii) both the greatest and the least elements of $L^*(y)$ are increasing in y.

To use these results for proving the existence of a Nash equilibrium for a supermodular game, note that they directly apply to the maximization of a supermodular function rather than the minimization of a submodular function.[13] Further, the theorem requires that the objective function be upper semicontinuous, implying that jumps of payoffs only in the upward direction are allowed.[14] Given this condition on the payoff functions for the supermodular game, Topkis's result implies that the best response correspondences for each player are nonempty and form a sublattice.

The fact that the best response set is a sublattice is an almost immediate consequence of the fact that the payoff function is assumed to be supermodular. In particular, suppose x and y are both elements of player i's best response correspondence, $br_i(s_{-i})$. Then the supermodularity of the payoff function implies that

---

13. The minimization of a submodular function is equivalent to the maximization of the negative of that function, which is supermodular.
14. Formally, a function $f(x)$ is upper semicontinuous at x if $\lim_{x_n \to x} f(x_n) \le f(x)$.

$$0 \geq \sigma_i(x \wedge y, s_{-i}) - \sigma_i(x, s_{-i}) \geq \sigma_i(y, s_{-i}) - \sigma_i(x \vee y, s_{-i}) \geq 0$$

The first and last inequalities hold since x and y are both elements of the best response correspondence. The middle one holds, because of the assumption of supermodularity. The consequence of this (as in Topkis [1978, Theorem 4.1]) is that the best response correspondence must be a sublattice of the strategy space. That is, if x and y are elements of $br_i(s_{-i})$, then so will their meet and their join.

Further, Topkis's theorem implies that there are least and greatest elements in the best response correspondence which are monotone functions of the actions of other players, s_{-i}.[15] It is in this sense that the set of optimal actions of one player are increasing in the strategies of the others. This is an important property from the individual optimization side of the equilibrium analysis since it will provide the basic function for the fixed point argument.

To prove the existence of a Nash equilibrium, we combine the results from Topkis with the fixed point theorem of Tarski. To proceed, let $\underline{br}_i(s_{-i})$ be the least element of $br_i(s_{-i})$, which we now know exists and is increasing in s_{-i} from Topkis's theorem. Let $\underline{br}(s) \in s$ for $s \in S$ be the vector of the least element of best responses for each player. Since this is an increasing function, we can immediately use this to prove the existence of a Nash equilibrium by employing Tarski's fixed point theorem. This gives the minimal element in the set of Nash equilibria for the supermodular game. One can also select the greatest element in the best response correspondence for each player and use Topkis's theorem to show that this is also monotone. Again, employing Tarski's fixed point theorem gives the maximal element in the set of Nash equilibria.

Figures 2.5–2.7 illustrate the existence result. For the game in Figure 2.5, there are two elements in the strategy set, $\{(0, 0), (1, 1)\}$. To simplify, assume that there are two players with identical payoffs and the same strategy sets. Suppose that the best response of one player to $(0, 0)$ is $\{(0, 0), (1, 1)\}$ while the best response to $(1, 1)$ is $(1, 1)$. By symmetry, these are also the best responses of the other player. The arrows in these figures indicate the *maximal* elements of the best response of one player (the head of the arrow) to an action of the other (the base of the arrow). So, in Figure 2.5, the maximal best response of the representative player is $(1, 1)$ for both $(0, 0)$ and $(1, 1)$. Note that this game satisfies the condition for Tarski's fixed point theorem as the strategy space for each player is

---

15. Formally, one can prove this by contradiction using the assumed property of increasing first differences.

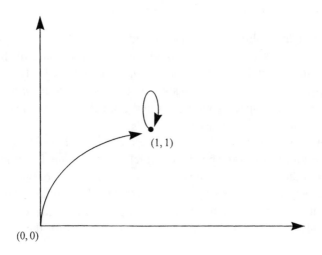

Figure 2.5

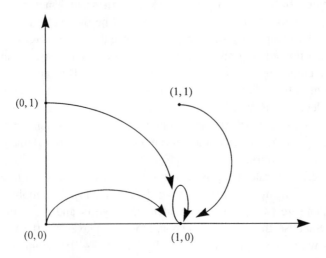

Figure 2.6

a complete lattice and the maximal best response function is increasing. In fact, (1, 1) is clearly a Nash equilibrium for this game. If instead we had chosen the least element of the best response correspondence, then (0, 0) would have been a fixed point.

Note too that if there is not a monotone selection out of the best response

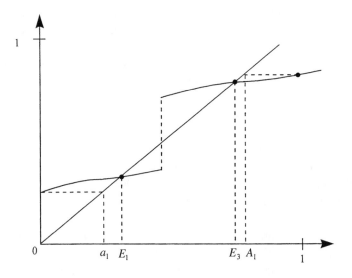

Figure 2.7

correspondence, then it is easy to see that an equilibrium may not exist. In particular, suppose that the unique best response to $(0, 0)$ is $(1, 1)$ and the unique best response to $(1, 1)$ is $(0, 0)$. In this case, the best response function is not monotone and no pure strategy equilibrium exists.

Figure 2.6 illustrates a slightly more complicated strategy space to illustrate further the fixed point argument. Again, we consider a symmetric supermodular game with two players where the greatest elements of the best response correspondence for a single player are shown in the figure. Note that either $(0, 0)$ is a fixed point or $(0, 0)$ is never a best response, a feature of these games that we return to later in our discussion of iterative deletion in supermodular games. Similarly, $(1, 1)$ either is a fixed point or is never a best response. When $(0, 0)$ and $(1, 1)$ are not fixed points, then the best responses to these strategies must be higher (lower) than these points, as indicated by the arrows in Figure 2.6. As long as the best responses satisfy the monotonicity property implied by Topkis's theorem, there will always exist a fixed point as indicated in the figure.[16] Here, in the symmetric equilibrium both players choose strategy $(1, 0)$.

16. The key implication of the theorem is that, for example, the best response to $(1, 1)$ must be no less than the best responses to $(0, 1)$, $(1, 0)$ or $(0, 0)$. Note that the point is not that the best response to, say, $(1, 0)$ must exceed $(1, 0)$ but rather that the response to $(1, 1)$ cannot be less than that to $(1, 0)$.

Figure 2.7 illustrates the case where each player has a best response function which maps from an interval of the real line, [0, 1], into that same interval as in the Cooper–John model described earlier. The figure displays the best response function for one of the two identical players. Note that the best response of the player to 0 is to take an action greater than 0 and the best response to 1 is less than 1. Further, the best response function is not continuous but is still increasing as the jump is upward. Clearly there are two pure strategy Nash equilibria for this game, E_1 and E_3, as well as a mixed strategy equilibrium.

One very important point is not covered by these results: the nature of the equilibrium set. As stressed by Vives [1990], these results on the existence of a Nash equilibrium are not informative about the structure of the entire set of equilibria. The Tarski fixed point theorem told us only that the set of fixed points was a complete lattice for *some* function f, for which we took either the maximal or the minimal elements of the best response correspondence. This result guarantees that an equilibrium will exist, but it does not tell us that the set of equilibria has any particular structure, such as being a lattice.

Suppose we strengthen the restrictions on payoffs to consider a strictly supermodular game in which we assume strictly increasing first differences and strict supermodularity. Then, according to Topkis, the reaction correspondence for an individual player is ordered by the actions of others and the set of Nash equilibria is a nonempty sublattice. Further, Vives [1990, Theorem 4.1 and Theorem 4.2] argues that the set of Nash equilibria for a strictly supermodular game is a complete sublattice.

Iterative Deletion and the Convergence of the Best Response Dynamics

As noted by Milgrom and Roberts, equilibria of supermodular games have an interesting relationship to the concept of dominance solvability and the process of iteratively deleting strongly dominated strategies. A strategy for player i, s_i, is strongly dominated if, for all s_{-i}, the payoff from selecting s_i is less than the payoff from selecting some other feasible strategy.

Consider an iterative process which, starting with the set of feasible strategy combinations S, eliminates strongly dominated strategies for each player in the set I of players. At each step in the process, a strategy is eliminated for player i if it is strongly dominated by another strategy for *i* for all strategy combinations which have not been eliminated in previous steps of the iteration process. Milgrom and Roberts prove the following:

> **Theorem 2 (Milgrom–Roberts [1990]).** *Let* Γ *be a supermodular game. For each player i, there exist largest and smallest serially undominated strategies* $\bar{x}_i$ *and* $\underline{x}_i$. *Moreover, the strategy profiles* $(\underline{x}_i;$ *i* $\in$ *I) and* $(x_i;$ *i* $\in$ *I) are pure Nash equilibrium profiles.*

In this theorem, serially undominated strategies are those that are not eliminated through the iterative deletion process described. Since strategy sets are ordered, the set of serially undominated strategies has largest and smallest elements. The theorem is that the strategy profiles constructed with these largest (smallest) strategies are Nash equilibria.

The games exhibited in Figures 2.6 and 2.7 provide some insights into these results. To simplify the discussion, assume for both that best responses are unique and are as indicated in the figures. As discussed, in the Figure 2.6 game, (1, 1) is not a best response to (1, 1). Hence, (1, 1) must be a dominated strategy: otherwise the best response function would not be increasing. Therefore, using symmetry, (1, 1) can be eliminated from the strategy space under consideration for both players. By a similar argument, (0, 0) can be eliminated as well. Finally, (0, 1) is dominated by (1, 0). This leaves the unique equilibrium in which (1, 0) is chosen by both players.

In the Figure 2.7 example, the first round of deletion will eliminate all strategies below the point a_1 and all strategies above A_1 since elements below and above these points, respectively, are dominated. After trimming the strategy space to $[a_1, A_1]$ we find that the strategies in the intervals $[a_1, a_2)$ and $(A_2, A_1]$ are dominated. Note that these strategies were not eliminated in the first round as they were best responses to the strategies in either $[0, a_1)$ or $(A_1, 1]$. Continuation of this iterative deletion leads to the elimination of strategies below E_1 and above E_3, the greatest and least elements in the set of Nash equilibria.

To see one important implication of iterative deletion, suppose that there is a unique equilibrium for the supermodular game. In this case, Milgrom and Roberts show that the equilibrium is dominance solvable: i.e., the equilibrium outcome is the only strategy combination left after the iterative deletion process. This is true for the example in Figure 2.6. Is it reasonable to expect players to coordinate play on this equilibrium? Since a dominance solvable equilibrium is achievable through the iterated deletion of dominated strategies, it is quite reasonable to think that players will proceed to "find" such a equilibrium. In particular, one does not require the common knowledge of rationality to achieve this equilibrium.

When there are multiple equilibria in a supermodular game, as in the example at the start of this section and in Figure 2.7, then the dominance solvability argument loses some strength. In this case, one can still proceed to delete some strategies, but the outcome of iterative deletion will, of course, not lead to a selection from the set of equilibria. The issues of selection in supermodular games with multiple equilibria are discussed further later.

The greatest and least elements in the set of Nash equilibria are also the outcomes of a well-known process of best response dynamics, the Cournot tatonnemont. In this process, the outcome in iteration n is a selection from the best response correspondence to the vector of strategies selected from the iteration $n-1$ correspondence. That is, starting with $s_0 \in S$, $a_n \in br(a_{n-1})$ where $br(s)$ is the best response correspondence to $s \in S$. Vives [1990, Theorem 5.1] proves that if the process starts with s_0 greater (less) than the largest (smallest) Nash equilibrium, the Cournot tatonnemont will converge to the greatest (smallest) Nash equilibrium.

Figure 2.7 again illustrates. For any s_0 below E_1, the best response exceeds s_0. Thus the iterative process is a strictly increasing function that clearly converges to E_1. A similar statement holds above the largest Nash equilibrium E_3.

Welfare

One of the important results in the Cooper–John analysis was the fact that the Nash equilibria were Pareto-ordered by the level of activity. That type of result carries over to supermodular games. The important condition for this result is again *positive spillovers:* payoffs to any player increase if the strategy choice by any other player is increased. In the case of differentiable payoff functions, in contrast to the concept of supermodularity (strategy complementaries), positive spillovers are a first derivative property of the payoff function and not a restriction on the cross-partial of the payoff function.

Suppose that both x and y are strategy combinations in S and are Nash equilibria with $x > y$. Milgrom and Roberts ([1990], Theorem 7) prove that if $\sigma_i(s_i, s_{-i})$ is increasing in s_{-i} for all $i \in I$, then $\sigma_i(x) > \sigma_i(y)$ for all players. Intuitively, start at equilibrium y and suppose that all players except i increase their strategy to x_j ($j \neq i$). From the assumption of positive spillovers, player i is better off. Since $x_i \in br_i(x_i)$, player i must be better off in the equilibrium where x is the strategy combination since he could have chosen y_i.

Comparative Statics

A final important aspect of the Cooper–John example was the presence of a multiplier effect and more generally the monotone nature of the comparative statics. For a variety of macroeconomic applications, it is important to see how the equilibrium (or set of equilibria) moves in response to changes in the environment. As we see later, one macroeconomic implication of this class of games is the propagation over time and across agents of exogenous changes to the underlying environment. Supermodular games, by their restrictions on payoff functions, have built into them the basis for positive comovement in activity across agents, which is also an important characteristic of business cycles.

To understand this, parameterize the game by θ and suppose that θ lies in a partially ordered set. Then introduce θ into payoffs so that $\sigma_i(s, \theta)$ and assume that this function exhibits increasing first differences in s_i and θ given s_{-i}. Theorem 6 and its corollary in Milgrom and Roberts show that the set of Nash equilibria varies in a particular way with changes in θ. In particular, they find that the largest and smallest pure Nash equilibria are nondecreasing functions of θ. Note that this does not imply that all of the Nash equilibria are increasing in θ. For example, in the economy given in Figure 2.1, an increase in θ such that the reaction curve shifts upward will increase the lowest and highest but not the middle equilibrium.

SUMMARY

The goal of this chapter was to provide a general structure for coordination games. The key characteristic of these games is the presence of strategic complementarities, essentially a monotonicity property of best responses. It is possible for supermodular games to have multiple equilibria which, in the presence of positive spillovers, can be Pareto-ordered. This gives some content to the notion of a coordination failure. The results from Cooper and John [1988] supplement the more general results by focusing on a special class of games.

This discussion should provoke two key questions. First, are coordination failures a theoretical curiosity, or is there some evidence that they actually might arise? This question has already been addressed in the previous chapter, where we reported on some recent experimental evidence concerning the possibility of coordination failures. This evidence suggests that the Pareto-dominant Nash equilibrium does not serve as a focal point for all coordination games.

Second, and from the perspective of macroeconomics this is the most important question, are there economies that, at least qualitatively, can be represented as a supermodular game? The goal of the next chapters is to address this question in some detail.

3 Technological Complementarities

We begin the study of economic environments underlying coordination games by considering the most direct form of interaction across agents: through a production function. As we shall see, this simple structure forms the basis for new insights into both aggregate economic fluctuations and growth. Further, this source of complementarity is most tractable in terms of quantitative analysis since it is most easily incorporated into the stochastic growth model.

Consequently, the discussion in this chapter contains both theory and quantitative evidence associated with the behavior of these economies. This focus reflects, in fact, recent developments in quantitative analysis which allow us to go beyond the stochastic growth model studied by Kydland and Prescott [1982] and King, Plosser and Rebelo [1988] to understand macroeconomic dynamics of economies with distortions.

INPUT GAMES AND TECHNOLOGICAL COMPLEMENTARITY

Assume that I agents provide effort into a joint production process. The per capita output of this process is $f(e_1, e_2, \ldots, e_I)$ where e_i is the effort level of agent i in the production process. We assume that $e \in [0, 1]$ so that the strategy space is a complete lattice. Per capita output is also the consumption for each agent. Implicit here is an assumption about the nature of the compensation scheme: agents share equally in the output from their joint production.

41

Let $U(c_i)$ be the utility from goods consumption and $g(e_i)$ be the disutility of effort for agent i. Hence

$$\sigma(e_i, e) = U(f(e_1, e_2, \ldots, e_I)) - g(e_i) \tag{1}$$

Assume that $U(\cdot)$ is strictly increasing and concave and that $g(\cdot)$ is strictly increasing and strictly convex.

In analyzing the game between agents, the key assumption will concern the nature of their interaction through the joint production process. These interactions may arise internally within a firm or through some form of external economy. For the purposes of this discussion, it might be best to think of this as a problem within a firm. We return to alternative interpretations and uses of this structure in macroeconomic models later in the chapter.

Internal Returns to Scale

Suppose first that there are increasing returns which are internal to the production process. That is, let per capita output equal $f(\sum_j e_j)$ where $f(\cdot)$ is strictly increasing and strictly convex. To simplify, assume $U(c) = c$. The reaction curve for agent i, when all other agents choose effort level E, is given implicitly by the effort level, e, that solves

$$f'(e + (I - 1)E) = g'(e)$$

As long as $f''(e + (I - 1)E) - g''(e) < 0$, so that the increasing returns in production are offset by the curvature in the disutility of effort function, the second-order condition will be met.

Strategic complementarities occur if the optimal effort level of an agent is increasing in the effort levels of the others: i.e., iff $(de/dE) > 0$. From the first-order condition, this derivative is given by

$$\frac{f''(e + (I-1)E)(I-1)}{-(f''(e + (I-1)E) - g''(e))} > 0 \tag{2}$$

So strategic complementarity, assuming the second-order condition is satisfied, is equivalent to increasing returns to scale in this model. In words, increased effort by all other agents will increase the productivity of the remaining agent, thus inducing more effort on his part as well.

The condition for a symmetric Nash equilibrium at effort level e is

$$f'(Ie) - g'(e) = 0 \tag{3}$$

Assuming that $g'(0) = 0$ and $g'(1) = \infty$, the conditions that $f'(0) > 0$ and $f'(I) < \infty$ will ensure the existence of an interior Nash equilibrium. In some cases, such as the example given later, multiple Nash equilibria are possible. Since there are positive spillovers in this economy (when others work harder, per capita consumption is higher), if there are multiple symmetric Nash equilibria, they will be Pareto-ranked.

External Returns

An alternative approach emphasizes returns to scale that are completely external to a particular agent. In this case, the returns to scale are created by the effects of other agents outside an internal constant returns to scale production process.

To generate numerous examples, assume that $U(c) = c$, $g(e) = (e^2/2\gamma)$ and $c = ef(E)$ where E is the average level of output by the other agents. So here there are constant returns to scale for the individual agent and, assuming that $f'(\cdot) > 0$, there are social increasing returns to scale. The first-order condition for the individual's choice of effort satisfies $e = \gamma f(E)$. From this, reaction curves with multiple crossings are quite easy to generate using an appropriately chosen form for the function $f(E)$.

The Min Example

An illuminating example which also emphasizes the possibility of multiple equilibria comes from Bryant [1983], where $f(e_1, e_2, \ldots e_I) = \min (e_1, e_2, \ldots e_I)$. In this technology, the level of effort by each agent is important for the determination of per capita output. As in a production line process, one "bad apple" can have a large impact regardless of the length of the line.

Let $\bar{e}$ solve $U'(\bar{e}) = g'(\bar{e})$. The level of effort $\bar{e}$ represents the cooperative solution (the effort level that maximizes joint utility) to the team production problem with this technology.

In this game, $e_i = \bar{e}$ for all i is a symmetric Nash equilibrium. To see why, first note that there is no additional production from increasing effort due to the specific technology. Second, the agent's utility falls from reduced effort since $\bar{e}$ is the cooperative effort level. Hence, if all others choose $\bar{e}$ so will an arbitrary agent. Note that this argument uses the fact that if an agent chooses an effort level below all others, then that agent's payoff is determined by that action.

As pointed out by Bryant, there is in fact a continuum of symmetric Nash equilibria in this game. Any $e_i = e \in [0, \bar{e}]$ for $i = 1, 2, \ldots I$ is an equilibrium. For any such e, agents cannot gain by increasing their own effort and lose by reducing effort (since $U'(\bar{e}) > g'(\bar{e})$ for $e < \bar{e}$). Again, by putting forth less effort than others, the agent determines his payoffs, and thus putting forth less effort is not desirable because of the strict concavity of the function $U(e) - g(e)$. Since $U(e) - g(e)$ is strictly increasing for $e \in [0, \bar{e}]$, these equilibria are Pareto-ordered.

This represents a severe case of multiple equilibria in that the set of Nash equilibria forms a continuum so that an equilibrium outcome is not locally unique. The economy can become stuck at an inefficient equilibrium. All agents recognize that preferred equilibria exist but none, acting alone, can coordinate economic activity.

Because of the simplicity of this team production problem, there are ways out of this dilemma through changes in the incentive scheme. That is, the coordination problems arising here are (partly) a consequence of the rule that distributes output equally to all agents regardless of their effort levels. In particular, if effort levels of all agents are observable, one could design a contract with large penalties that would lead each agent to choose effort level $\bar{e}$. Even if individual efforts were not observed, since there is no uncertainty in this environment, a contract which penalized agents if per capita output did not equal $\bar{e}$ would be equally effective.[1] The important point to recognize is that coordination problems emerge in strategic settings where there are imperfections in the contracting process and/or incompleteness of markets.

A discrete version of this economy underlies the experimental work of van Huyck et al. cited in Chapter 1. From the perspective of that paper, the multiple equilibria that emerge in a discrete version of the Bryant model are not simply a technical curiosity: coordination failures can and do arise in experimental settings.

One point raised in those experiments reemerges in this example: the role of the number of agents.[2] Consider an economy with $I = 2$. Each agent can choose $e \in \{0, 1\}$ and has preferences given by $c - (\gamma/2)e^2$. Further, assume that the technology combined with a distribution of output across agents implies $c = \min(e_1, e_2)$. So far, this is just a discrete version of the Bryant example.

---

1. See Holmstrom [1982] for a more complete discussion of team incentive problems.
2. This discussion draws upon Jovanovic [1987].

Suppose the disutility of effort, denoted by γ, is random. In particular, assume that with probability π, agent $i = 1$, 2 has a value of γ, denoted γ_h, which exceeds 2. In this case, putting forth effort of 0 is a dominant strategy. With probability $(1 - \pi)$, the realized value of γ, denoted γ_l, is less than 2. Agents' types are independently drawn and actions are selected without knowing the other agent's type.

For this economy of two agents, there are two equilibria. In one, both agents choose effort level 1 whenever their realized value of γ is γ_l and choose zero effort otherwise. As long as π is sufficiently low, this behavior is optimal given that the other player is pursuing the same strategy. Of course, the second equilibrium has zero effort for both agent types.

Now suppose that the number of agents increases. The equilibrium in which all agent types choose zero effort will remain an equilibrium regardless of the number of agents. However, for a large enough set of agents, the equilibrium in which an agent chooses effort of 1 when γ_l is realized will no longer exist. The argument is simple. For fixed π, as the number of agents increases the probability that *one* of the others will draw $\gamma = \gamma_h$ increases as well. Given the min technology, this makes the choice of the high effort level untenable.

BUSINESS CYCLE IMPLICATIONS

In this section of the chapter, we discuss attempts to build stochastic, dynamic versions of the more static coordination models. We begin by discussing a paper by Baxter and King [1991] which, except for the addition of a technological complementarity, bears a close resemblance in structure, though not in results, to the standard real business cycle model. We then examine recent work on sunspot equilibria and dynamic complementarities.

Imagine an economy composed of a large number of infinitely lived individuals all solving for consumption, employment and capital accumulation paths in the classical one-sector growth model. This model provides the basis for the real business cycle model, explored by Kydland and Prescott [1982], King, Plosser and Rebelo [1988] and numerous others. Suppose further that the production function for each agent has the usual arguments of capital and labor as well as an exogenous technological parameter and, most importantly, a technological external complementarity.

Formally consider the problem of a representative household:

$$\max\ E_0 \sum_0^\infty \beta^t u(c_t + \Delta_t,\ l_t) \tag{4}$$

subject to:

$$l_t + n_t \le 1 \tag{5}$$

$$c_t + i_t \le y_t \tag{6}$$

$$k_{t+1} = k_t(1-\delta) + i_t \tag{7}$$

and

$$y_t = A_t F(k_t,\ n_t)(Y_t)^\varepsilon \tag{8}$$

In the objective function, the period utility function is defined over consumption and leisure and is strictly increasing and strictly concave and the discount rate β lies between 0 and 1. The expectation is taken with respect to the stochastic taste disturbance (Δ_t) and the technology parameter (A_t). The variable Δ_t is a parameter which influences the period t marginal rate of substitution between consumption and leisure.

The first constraint indicates that the agent has a unit endowment of time in each period which can be enjoyed as leisure or used as an input into the production process (n_t). The second constraint is the resource constraint: output can either be consumed or be used as gross investment. The third constraint is the capital accumulation condition that relates the capital stock over time to gross investment where δ is the rate of capital depreciation.

Thus far, the model is quite standard.[3] The novelty of the model lies in the specification of the production function where the technological complementarity is present. In this last constraint of the optimization problem, output of the agent depends on the stock of capital, the labor input, the current state of technology (A_t), the current taste shock and a measure of average economywide output in period t, Y_t. The specification captures a technological spillover along the lines suggested by the work of Bryant [1983] and one that has appeared in growth models with externalities in the capital accumulation process. In contrast to the Bryant formulation, the technological spillover does not depend on the inputs of others but rather the level of output. This is taken to be a metaphor for the view that individuals are more productive in periods of high economic activity.

---

3. There is also a government in the Baxter–King formulation which taxes net output at a fixed rate, purchases a constant amount of goods and transfers goods back to agents. The government is ignored in this presentation.

Importantly, it is possible to estimate the magnitude of this spillover, as described later.

The individual agent is assumed to be small and thus takes the actions of others as given in his own optimization problem. Note that this is more than the usual Nash equilibrium assumption: the agent thinks he has no influence on the state of the economy in the future.

The first-order conditions for an individual agent are given by:

$$u_1(c_t + \Delta_t, l_t) = \lambda_t \tag{9}$$

$$u_2(c_t + \Delta_t, l_t) = \lambda_t A_t F_2(k_t, n_t)(Y_t)^\varepsilon \tag{10}$$

and

$$\beta E \lambda_{t+1}[A_{t+1}F_1(k_{t+1}, n_{t+1})(Y_{t+1})^\varepsilon + (1-\delta)] = \lambda_t \tag{11}$$

The first two conditions ensure that the agent is optimizing in terms of the static allocation of labor time in a given time period: i.e., these are conditions of intratemporal optimality. The third condition is an intertemporal optimality condition relating the marginal utility of consumption in period t to expected product of the return to holding capital and the marginal utility of consumption in period $t + 1$. Note that in deriving these conditions, the agent takes the aggregate level of output as given. These conditions along with the resource constraints and the condition for a symmetric equilibrium, given later, describe the path of the economy.

Before proceeding further, we adopt some of the additional restrictions used by Baxter and King. First, assume the $F(k, n)$ is a Cobb–Douglas function: i.e., $F(k, n) = k^\theta n^{(1-\theta)}$. Second, assume that the utility function is given by $u(c + \Delta, 1) = \log(c + \Delta) + \chi\log(l)$. These assumptions are made to allow tractability and to ensure that the model matches up with some key moments of U.S. data.[4]

This economy is a dynamic game in that the optimal choices of a single agent, through the first-order conditions given, depend on the evolution of aggregate output. But aggregate output itself is determined by the average behavior of the agents. Thus solving this problem requires both the solution of an individual's dynamic optimization problem and the characterization of an equilibrium in terms of decision rules. The symmetry in the economy greatly aids the second of these operations, as we shall see.

---

4. In particular, King, Plosser and Rebelo point out that this specification is necessary to match the observation that neither the real interest rate nor the average amount of hours worked appears to have a trend.

Let the state contingent level of per capia output be given by $Y(A, \Delta, K)$, where K is the average capital stock in the economy. The evolution of K is governed by some state dependent policy function, $H(\cdot)$, such that the future value of K is given by $H(A, \Delta, K)$. Solution of the individual's intertemporal optimization problem will yield decision rules, $y(A, \Delta, k)$ and $h(A, \Delta, k)$, for output and capital accumulation, respectively.

Since there are no differences across agents, an equilibrium arises when the individual and aggregate decision rules coincide. That is, we use $y(A, \Delta, k) = Y(A, \Delta, K)$, $h(A, \Delta, k) = H(A, \Delta, K)$ and $K = k$ in all states as conditions for a symmetric equilibrium. With the Cobb–Douglas production function, $y = Y$ implies that $y = [Ak^\theta n^{1-\theta}]^\eta$ where $\eta \equiv (1/(1 - \varepsilon))$. Thus if $0 < \varepsilon < 1$, then $\eta > 1$ and the economy will exhibit external returns to scale.

With these specified functions, and using the condition of a symmetric equilibrium, the necessary conditions given previously become

$$\frac{1}{c + \Delta} = \lambda(A, \Delta, k) \tag{12}$$

$$\frac{1}{1 - n} = \lambda(A, \Delta, k)(1 - \theta)[Ak^\theta n^{(1-\theta)}]^\eta/n \tag{13}$$

and

$$\beta E\lambda(A', \Delta', k')\left[\frac{\theta}{k'}(A'k'^\theta n'^{(1-\theta)})^\eta + (1 - \delta)\right] = \lambda(A, \Delta, k) \tag{14}$$

where the future variables are indicated by primes. A stationary equilibrium is given by state contingent consumption, employment, investment decisions plus a state contingent Lagrange multiplier that satisfies these conditions as well as the resource constraint, for all (A, Δ, k).

From these conditions, it is critical to note that in equilibrium individual marginal products of labor (13) and capital (14) have a social increasing returns component. This comes about from the condition of symmetric Nash equilibrium within any period so that $y_t = [A_t F(k_t, n_t)]^\eta$. These conditions are quite similar to those emerging from the one-sector growth model, as in King, Plosser and Rebelo, except for the η multiplying the parameters of the Cobb–Douglas technology.

These first-order conditions can be used to characterize a steady state where both taste and technology shocks are absent. Then, as in King, Plosser and Rebelo, Baxter and King use a log-linear approximation of these conditions for the stochastic economy around the steady state, yielding a linear system in the state variables, $s = (k, A, \Delta)$, where these variables should now be interpreted as percentage deviations from the steady state.[5]

With this linear approximation, the analysis is reduced to following the progress of the state vector. To do so requires a specification of the underlying stochastic processes for tastes and technology and, in order to obtain quantitative predictions, the parameterization of the model. Once the evolution of the state vector is known, other variables of interest (such as consumption, employment, productivity, investment and output) are computed using the linear decision rules.

The sector vector evolves according to $s' = Ms + \xi$ where $\xi = [0, a, d]$ represents the current innovations to the tastes and technology processes. The first element of the innovation vector is zero since the capital accumulation process is not stochastic. The matrix M reflects the decision rule which relates the future capital stock to the state vector and the serial correlation in the technology and taste shocks, ρ_A and ρ_Δ:

$$M = \begin{pmatrix} \mu_1 & \pi_{KA} & \pi_{K\Delta} \\ 0 & \rho_A & 0 \\ 0 & 0 & \rho_\Delta \end{pmatrix} \tag{15}$$

In this matrix, the first row relates the future value of k to the current values of the state variable where the constants μ_1, π_{KA} and π_{KA} are determined from the equilibrium decision rules. It is precisely these coefficients that capture the effects of preferences and technology on the evolution of the capital stock and its response to the shocks.[6] Note that there is assumed to be some serial correlation in the shocks to both technology and tastes, ρ_A and ρ_Δ, respectively.

The next step is parameterization of the model. Following the real business cycle tradition, the parameters of preferences and some of the parameters determining the technology are determined from long-run observations on the economy and related econometric studies. For example, the parameters for the technology are set with capital's share, φ, at .42. The processes for the exogenous technology shock are obtained as Solow

---

5. Consumption is effectively eliminated from the system using the condition for saddle path stability.
6. The interested reader can produce these elements of this matrix through the linearization procedure. The appendix to King, Plosser and Rebelo is a very helpful source for this type of exercise.

residuals from the appropriate production function. In particular, one must be careful to recognize that the inferred productivity series will be dependent upon the existence of social returns to scale. Baxter and King find that in the specification with external increasing returns the standard deviation of the technology shock is only about 80% of that in the more standard case of constant returns. For both cases, they are unable to reject the presence of a unit root in the technology process.

The novel elements for this study are the technology spillover parameter and the structure of the demand shock process. For the former, Baxter and King use an instrumental variables estimation routine to identify the spillover parameters using aggregate data. The instruments chosen are arguably independent of any technology shock in the economy. From this, they set ε at .23 and hence η at 1.3, which is close to related estimates provided by Caballero and Lyons [1992].[7]

In contrast to the standard business cycle model, this construct includes a disturbance to the marginal utility of consumption. In order to calibrate the model, this process must be parameterized. To do so, Baxter and King use the intratemporal first-order condition relating the marginal rate of substitution between consumption and leisure to the marginal product of labor. By assuming that the marginal product of labor is proportional to the real wage, the taste shock can be inferred from observations on consumption, employment and the real wage.[8]

Given this model, there are at least two interesting exercises. First, what are the implications of demand shocks? Second, does the introduction of technological complementarities into the basic growth model improve its ability to mimic key features of the business cycle?

Using the model with *external returns to scale and taste shocks* alone, Baxter and King report that the model produces (i) positively correlated fluctuations in the key components of aggregate gross national product (GNP), (ii) fluctuations which are persistent in terms of deviations from trend and (iii) consumption which is less volatile than output, which is, in turn, less volatile than investment. These are the same features that are

---

7. Cooper and Haltiwanger [1996] describe the estimation issues in some detail and discuss an attempt by Braun and Evans [1991] to estimate this parameter using seasonal data. The use of seasonal data is a natural way to identify the social returns to scale since one would generally not argue that seasonal fluctuations are predominantly due to technology shocks. See also Basu and Fernald [1995] for an argument that the estimated returns to scale reflect the use of value added as an output measure. Cooper and Johri [1997] provide further evidence in support of complementarities in the production process.

8. For the discussion that follows, it is important to note that the estimated taste shock is highly serially correlated.

prominently displayed by models which are driven by technology shocks. The novelty of the Baxter–King exercise is that quite similar implications arise in models with demand shocks *if* there are external increasing returns to scale.

To understand this point better, Baxter and King feed the same demand disturbances through the model in which there are no increasing returns and no technology shocks. Not surprisingly, the predictions of the model become inconsistent with central features of the business cycle. In particular, consumption becomes much more volatile than investment and investment is negatively correlated with output. This reflects the fact that in periods of (temporary) high marginal utility, production and consumption will increase and investment will fall to satisfy the intertemporal optimality condition. Finally, output volatility is much less in the model with constant returns since the external returns to scale model magnifies the effects of the demand disturbance.

Despite these dimensions of success, both of these models produce predictions concerning the relationship between productivity and output which are counterfactual. Even in the presence of external returns to scale, it appears that demand shocks give rise to countercyclical movements in productivity. Given the specification of technology, the average product of labor is given by

$$A^\eta k^{\theta\eta} n^{(1-\theta)\eta-1} \tag{16}$$

Hence increases in n will cause the average product of labor to fall as long as $(1 - \theta)\eta < 1$, which is true for the parameterization of the model with $\theta = .42$ and $\eta = 1.3$. Note that if $(1 - \theta)\eta > 1$, either because of a larger labor share or a larger complementarity, then productivity will be positively related to the level of employment. From society's perspective, it is as if labor demand were increasing in the level of employment, though, of course, labor demand is downward sloping for each individual firm. This is a point we return to in the discussion of sunspot equilibria.

In relation to the second exercise, Baxter and King consider a model in which both technology and preference shocks are present. This also permits an evaluation of the relative importance of preference and technology shocks in their model.[9]

Baxter and King find that the model with increasing returns, combined

---

9. As Baxter and King point out, uncovering the Solow residual is influenced by the magnitude of the increasing returns. This difference alone leads them to argue that the productivity shock has a smaller variance in the increasing returns setting.

with the inferred productivity and taste shocks, explains more of the variations in output than does the constant returns model and matches better the observations on relative variabilities of consumption and investment.[10] Further, the introduction of demand disturbances allows the models to match the near zero correlation between hours and productivity better, though, again, the increasing returns model is closer to the data.

Overall, this approach of introducing a strategic complementarity, in the form of a production externality, into an otherwise standard real business cycle model is promising from two perspectives. First, it indicates possible directions of improvement for the modeling of aggregate fluctuations. In particular, the results indicate that the addition of external returns allows for the incorporation of preference variations without creating negative correlations between consumption and investment and without creating excess volatility in consumption. This then opens up the possibility of exploring the effects of more interesting "demand shocks."

Second, this paper indicates that the approach to macroeconomics, building upon the presence of strategic complementarities, is promising as well in that these models can be used for quantitative exercises. Baxter and King identified a specific complementarity in the production process, and their paper provides a vehicle for exploring the quantitative implications of this complementarity for aggregate variables.

Note too that the quantitative contribution of complementarities was to magnify preference shocks. This exercise did not make use of the possibility of multiple equilibria that may arise in models with complementarities. Further, the linkages across agents were static not dynamic, though one could argue, perhaps through a learning by doing model, that dynamic spillovers are equally relevant. We discuss these points in turn.

Benhabib and Farmer [1994] and Farmer and Guo [1994] consider versions of this economy in which the presence of social returns to scale alters the dynamics of the economy.[11] In particular, these papers argue that if the social returns are sufficiently large and labor supply sufficiently elastic, then the stability properties of the steady state dramatically change. In particular, Benhabib and Farmer [1994] argue that a necessary condition for indeterminacy is that the "labor demand" curve, taken to be the set of wage and employment combinations that satisfies the firm's first-order condition *in a symmetric equilibrium,* is more steeply sloped than labor

10. Again, the model with constant returns predicts too much volatility in consumption relative to investment.
11. Equivalently, they look at economies with large markups.

supply. So returning to our discussion of the effects of taste shocks on productivity, the condition for upward sloping "labor demand" is that $(1 - \theta)\eta > 1$. Hence these models require large labor shares as well as large complementarities in order to create the positive relationship between employment and productivity.

For the basic real business cycle and the parameterizations investigated by Baxter and King, the steady state was always saddle path stable. However, for larger values of ε, the steady state can become a sink. In this case, there are multiple paths (sequences of consumption and capital stocks) converging to the same steady state. In this event, it is then possible to randomize across these self-fulfilling paths to create endogenous uncertainty in the economy. The conditions for sunspot equilibria of this type are discussed by Benhabib and Farmer [1994] and recently reviewed by Farmer [1993] and Benhabib and Farmer [1997].

The contribution of Farmer and Guo [1994] is to investigate the quantitative implications of these sunspot equilibria. Here they find that the basic features of their economy mimic those found in actual data. In particular, the basic patterns of consumption smoothing, volatile investment and procyclical productivity emerge in their economy. This is true even though fluctuations are driven by a zero mean "error" term added to the Euler equation: i.e., a sunspot variable. Thus the underlying complementarity produces procyclical productivity as well as persistent movement in these variables. Moreover, for their economy, the roots of the matrix characterizing the evolution of the state vector are complex, implying that convergence is oscillatory.

Durlauf [1991] considers a dynamic model with complementarities which differs from the standard model in a couple of important respects. First, the models are dynamic in nature, allowing Durlauf to study the time series properties of his economies. Second, Durlauf introduces local complementarities so that only "neighboring" agents influence each other. Third, the interactions themselves are dynamic in that agents influence others over time and not contemporaneously. Over time, however, local links have more aggregate implications as the set of agents potentially influenced by activity at one point expands. Fourth, Durlauf assumes that agents have a discrete choice between two production possibilities. Durlauf finds that these local complementarities can create multiple equilibria in the absence of shocks. Further, he uses this structure to study the dynamic patterns of activity as agents switch between techniques of production, creating persistent effects of shocks.

A crude version of this structure is used by Cooper and Johri [1997] in a stochastic growth setting. In the Cooper–Johri model, the productivity of an agent is influenced by the level of activity of other agents both contemporaneously and in the previous period.

They consider an economy in which the representative agent solves the following dynamic optimization problem:

$$\max \quad E\sum_{t=0}^{\infty}\beta^t u(c_t - \Delta_t, 1-n_t)$$
$$s.t. \quad c_t + i_t \le y_t \tag{17}$$
$$k_{t+1} = (1-\delta)k_t + i_t$$
$$y_t = A_t n_t^{\alpha} k_t^{\phi} Y_t^{\varepsilon} Y_{t-1}^{\gamma}$$

where the notation is the same as in the earlier problem though the production function allows two forms of interactions across agents. The first is through the influence of current aggregate activity (Y_t) on the output of an individual producer (y_t), parameterized by ε. This is the complementarity that forms the basis of Baxter and King [1991]. The second influence is through lagged activity (Y_{t-1}) and is parameterized by γ. As in the earlier discussion, the agent takes all economywide variables as exogenous.

Note that in this formulation, the past level of output is another state variable in the system. Interesting dynamics can emerge from the interaction of the two state variables: physical capital and experience.

Cooper and Johri estimate the production function parameters using both sectoral and plant level data. Further, they follow Burnside, Eichenbaum and Rebelo [1995] by using electricity consumption as a proxy for capital services. In addition, they use innovations to nonborrowed reserves and the innovations to the federal funds rate as instruments for their estimation of sectoral production functions. Overall, they find support for both contemporaneous and dynamic complementarities. In particular, in a specification imposing constant returns to scale in own inputs, they estimate $\varepsilon = .24$ and $\gamma = .32$.

With these dynamic complementarities, Cooper and Johri find that iid shocks to both technology and taste can be propagated. As is well understood, an economy with no complementarities produces very little serial correlation in output when shocks are iid. However, when both complementarities are set at their estimated values, the standard deviation of output increases by a factor of almost 5 and the serial correlation in output increases to .95 from .02.

INTERMEDIATION

A final example of a technological externality, which also has a macroeconomics flavor, is associated with Bryant [1987] and Weil [1989]. As in the second example given earlier in this chapter, consider an economy with increasing returns external to the agent.

In particular, Weil considers a two-period model in which agents' preferences over consumption today and tomorrow are given by $u(c_1, c_2)$, where $u(\cdot)$ is strictly increasing and quasi-concave and $u_1(0, y) = \infty$ for $y > 0$. Individuals have an endowment e_t in each period of life and can store commodities at a rate R between the first and second periods. The key to the model is that while R is taken as given by an individual, it is assumed to be an increasing function of the average level of savings in the economy. As a consequence, the economy exhibits social increasing returns though there are constant returns at the individual level. The assumption that R is an increasing function is taken to capture the idea of some types of technological spillovers in the economy. Alternatively, as in the related paper by Bryant [1987], the process of intermediation may create social returns to scale due to the presence of fixed costs in the intermediation technology.

The individual agent solves

$$
\begin{aligned}
&\max_{c_1,\, c_2,\, i} u(c_1,\, c_2) \\
&\text{s.t.} \\
&\quad c_1 + i = e_1, \qquad c_2 = e_2 + iR \quad \text{and} \quad i \ge 0
\end{aligned}
\tag{18}
$$

where i represents the level of investment. Let $i(R)$ be the solution to this problem. Since R depends, through the storage technology, on the average level of storage, denoted by I, the solution to the individual's problem may be written as a function, denoted $\phi(I)$. The presence of strategic complementarity depends on the relationship between I and i through R. Since R is assumed to be increasing in I, as long as savings for the individual is an increasing function of R, the economy will exhibit strategic complementarities. As usual, symmetric Nash equilibria (denoted by i^*) will be fixed points of the function $\phi(i)$.

Weil establishes two results. First, if savings is a decreasing function of R, there will only be a unique equilibrium with $i^* > 0$. This is a consequence of the fact that when savings is a decreasing function of the interest rate, then the model exhibits strategic substitutability and thus uniqueness of interior equilibria. This is an interesting case as many papers in the literature on the existence of equilibria with sunspots in overlapping generations models, such as Azariadis [1981], require that savings fall as R increases. Since Weil's goal is to relate conditions for multiple equilibria to those for sunspots, this is an important point.

Second, if at $I = 0$, the constraint that $i \geq 0$ is binding for the individual, Weil finds that the economy will exhibit an even number of interior equilibria.[12] In this case, $\phi(0) = 0$ so there is always an autarkic equilibrium. Further, since the marginal utility of consumption in the first period goes to infinity as c_1 goes to 0, we know that $\phi(e_1) < e_1$. So, the best response function equals 0 for I near 0 and lies below I for I near e_1. Hence, this function crosses the 45° line an even number of times. In the event that multiple equilibria exist, Weil would argue that animal spirits or sunspots would play a role in selecting the outcome. From this perspective, models which generate multiple equilibria from strategic complementarities provide an alternative setting for sunspot equilibria. For our purposes, the example by Weil provides another interesting case of production externalities.

FINANCIAL FRAGILITY AND THE GREAT DEPRESSION

Cooper and Ejarque [1995] extend these models to explore the Great Depression period using a dynamic model with a complementarity in the intermediation process. The point of the paper is to model the Great Depression as a coordination failure arising from financial fragility. Besides its attempt to understand this important historical episode, the paper also provides a methodology for constructing the sunspot equilibria associated with dynamic coordination games.

To study these issues, Cooper and Ejarque specify a model in which confidence in the intermediation process plays a central role in the decision making of optimizing agents. Because of complementarities in the intermediation process, the economy can have multiple steady states as in the

---

12. Alternatively, if $\phi(R(0)) > 0$, then $i^* = 0$ will not be an equilibrium and generically there will be an odd number of equilibria.

Bryant and Weil static examples discussed earlier: there is either a relatively active (thick) or an inactive (thin) financial system. Once multiple steady states exist, it is relatively straightforward to construct sunspots as randomizations between allocations in the neighborhood of the two steady states. So, macroeconomic fluctuations are driven by periods of optimism and pessimism associated with the returns from financial intermediation. The resulting economy has a unique equilibrium in the given state of the system: i.e., given the capital stock and the sunspot variable, the outcome is completely determined.

Cooper and Ejarque characterize the equilibria of their model using a dynamic programming approach. Given the inherent nonlinearity in the underlying economy and the multiplicity of steady states, linearization is not a productive approach. Note, though, that the dynamic programming approach requires its own approximation since the state space must be discrete.

Since agents are assumed to be identical, the Nash equilibrium of this economy can be conveniently represented as the solution of a stochastic, dynamic programming problem where the strategic uncertainty is represented by a sunspot variable. The realizations of this sunspot variable provide a coordination mechanism for the agents. The fact that the sunspot matters, of course, reflects the underlying indeterminacy of actions, as in the Bryant and Weil papers.

Formally, let $V(k, \theta)$ represent the value function for a representative agent with capital k when the realization of the sunspot variable is φ. The value function solves

$$V(k, \theta) = \max_{I,n} U(f(k, n) - I, n) + \beta E_{\theta'|\theta} V(g(I, \theta) + k(1-\delta_k), \theta')$$

where

$$g(I, \theta) = \begin{cases} I(1 + \underline{r}) & \text{if } \theta = \theta_p \\ (I-F)(1 + \overline{r}) & \text{if } \theta = \theta_o \end{cases} \tag{19}$$

In this specification, the current utility payoff depends on current consumption and employment. Consumption equals current output less the investment in the accumulation of capital. The evolution of the capital stock reflects the undepreciated stock plus the new flows.

The effect of the sunspots, represented by θ, enters the problem through the accumulation equation, $g(I, \theta)$.[13] If $\theta = \theta_p$, depositors are pessimistic,

---

13. Note that at this point the model is observationally equivalent to a model in which there are fundamentals driving the returns to intermediated activities. We return to the point of how one can distinguish these models later in our discussion of confidence building measures.

deposit flows are low and the return from investment (in terms of future capital) is $(1 + \underline{r})$. If $\theta = \theta_0$, depositors are optimistic and deposits are large enough that the coalition pays a per capita fixed cost of intermediation (F) to obtain a marginal return $(1 + \bar{r})$. Naturally, $\bar{r} > \underline{r}$ so that the marginal return on investment is higher in the technology with the fixed cost. Thus it is new investment flows into physical capital that are influenced by the current state of intermediation.

There are a couple of interpretations of the specification of the accumulation technology. The first is that the specification is simply an approximation to the nonlinear relationship in the $R(I)$ function that is central to the Weil model. The second is in terms of a technology choice for the intermediation process. Here F is a fixed cost of project evaluation and monitoring. If deposit flows are low, then the most profitable intermediation process is to avoid the fixed cost and use an inefficient technique for project evaluation. This yields a low marginal return and is self-fulfilling if savings is an increasing function of the return to deposits. If deposit flows are high, then it may be profitable to pay the fixed cost and utilize the high return technology. Again, this can be self-fulfilling and a high level equilibrium is created.

To study the dynamic coordination problem through this dynamic programming approach, two points must be established. First, there must be a solution to Bellman's equation, (19). Cooper and Ejarque make reference to arguments in Stokey and Lucas [1989] that there is a solution to (19). This is not surprising given that the underlying economy is essentially the standard growth model with shocks to the capital accumulation process. The fact that these shocks are endogenous does not affect the solution to the individual's optimization problem.

The second issue is ensuring the existence of a sunspot equilibrium. There are three parameters that are exogenously determined: the fixed cost (F) and the two returns, $\bar{r}$ and $\underline{r}$. The condition for the pessimistic steady state equilibrium is immediate since, by assumption, no single agent can establish the intermediation process without the participation of others. Formally, this is simply a matter of selecting a large enough value for the fixed cost. To guarantee the optimistic steady state, F cannot be too large and the gap between the returns must be large enough. Cooper and Ejarque provide conditions such that this equilibrium exists as well, which include some restrictions on the state space of the capital stock.[14] Once the parame-

---

14. Outisde this space, one or the other form of saving may become a dominant strategy.

ters are such that multiple steady states exist, a sunspot equilibrium is then constructed as a randomization in the neighborhood of the steady states. That is, Cooper and Ejarque consider a transition matrix for the sunspot variable with diagonal elements close to 1.

The first-order conditions for the individual agent are given by

$$U_1 f_n = -U_2. \tag{20}$$

$$U_1(c, n) = \beta E_{\theta'|\theta} U_1(c', n') \left[f_k + \frac{(1 - \delta)}{(1 + r(\theta'))} \right] (1 + r(\theta)) \tag{21}$$

The first equation is the usual intratemporal optimality condition, which equates the marginal rate of substitution between consumption and work with the marginal product of labor. The second equation is the Euler equation, which, through the sunspot variable, is directly influenced by the state of expectations. Variations in confidence levels will directly affect the returns to investment today as well as the expected value of undepreciated capital in the next period.

To the extent that the return to investment influences the consumption/savings decision, confidence will also influence the current level of employment, through the intratemporal optimality condition. In particular, with a predetermined capital stock and no technology shock, consumption and employment will generally move in opposite directions.

Further, for this economy, variations in confidence will lead consumption and investment initially to move in opposite directions. Given the state of confidence, the policy function of the agent will dictate the transitional dynamics for capital. As in the more traditional growth model, if, say, the capital stock is below its steady state (given the sunspot variable), then the transition will entail high investment, high employment and low consumption relative to the steady state. So, even in the transition, consumption and investment are negatively related.[15]

Cooper and Ejarque undertake a quantitative analysis of their model by calibrating the underlying parameters of tastes and technology. Further, they set the returns on the investment activities such that the interest rate differential is 3% and set *F* to ensure multiple steady states. Given this parameterization, they numerically solve the dynamic programming prob-

---

15. Cooper and Corbae [1997] study an overlapping generations model in which intermediated activity provides the funding for firms' labor demand. In that model, some of this negative comovement disappears.

lem and simulate their economy. Finally, they compute statistics for their economy and compare to data from the U.S. interwar period.

In some respects the model does quite well. If the data is pooled across the regimes, the model's properties are quite similar, in many respects, to the standard real business cycle model: the major aggregate variables are all positively correlated with output and productivity is procyclical. Further, consumption is less volatile than output, while investment is more volatile than output. Finally, the economy exhibits serial correlation in output close to unity, reflecting persistence in the sunspot process.

Given the discussion earlier about the induced substitution between consumption and investment, it is not surprising that the model produces a negative correlation between these variables. Further, consumption and employment are predicted to be negatively correlated. Neither of these correlations is found in the data for this period. In this sense, the model in which fluctuations are driven by variations in the productivity of the intermediation process does not convincingly match observations over this period. Nonetheless, this exercise indicates the possibility of exploring the quantitative properties of models in which fluctuations are driven by self-fulfilling regime shifts in confidence.

SUMMARY

The goal of this chapter was to explore one class of models which exhibits complementarities. These contributions grow from Bryant [1983], in which the productivity of a single agent is postulated to depend on the effort levels of others. While Bryant's original specification resulted in a continuum of Nash equilibria, other specifications have been used to produce locally unique equilibria. Further, the assumption of complementarities in the production function has been used to study the intermediation process as well.

A second element of this chapter was to highlight the quantitative aspects of this research. Starting with the contributions of Baxter and King [1991] and Klenow [1990], researchers are now able to study the quantitative properties of model economies with complementarities. This is an important step in that it introduces some element of discipline into the modeling process (i.e., models must in some way confront the data).

4   Imperfect Competition and
       Demand Spillovers

In this chapter we study models of imperfect competition. These economies display complementarity from a very simple mechanism. If others in the economy are producing more output, then they will be spending more as well and this induces increased demand for the product of an individual producer. Generally, the response of the producer will be to increase output as well. The linkage across agents is thus the familiar income–expenditure relationship common to many "Keynesian" style models of price rigidities.[1] However, these interactions do not require price rigidities as they derive simply from the assumed normality of goods. In fact, this type of linkage across agents is present in general equilibrium models without any distortions whatsoever. As we shall see, though, these interactions are much more powerful in imperfectly competitive economies. In particular, the income–expenditure linkages can create multipliers and, when combined with nonconvexities in technology, can lead to multiple, Pareto-ranked equilibria.

The exact specification of market structure is, of course, quite important in any study of imperfect competition. Here we study two economies. The first is a multisensor economy in which there are a small number of firms producing an identical product in each sector. This is an interesting model in that it combines strategic substitutability (across firms in a given sector) with a complementarity across sectors.

The second economy is one of monopolistic competition. We use this

---

1. See Bénassy [1993a] and the references therein for a thorough review of the connections between models of imperfect competition and wage/price rigidities.

economy first to elaborate on the nature of welfare losses due to imperfect competition and second to study the effects of money in the presence of menu costs. The final section of the chapter discusses the quantitative analysis of the monopolistic competition model.

MULTISECTOR COURNOT–NASH MODELS

The next class of models we consider deviates from the standard general equilibrium model by allowing firms to have market power as sellers of goods. In particular, we follow Hart [1982], Weitzman [1982] and others and consider an economy with multiple sectors. Firms within a sector produce an identical product and choose output, taking as given the position of the industry demand curve, determined by the level of activity in other sectors, and the output level of other firms in their own sector.

As there are multiple firms within each sector, this economy exhibits a rich set of interactions. As in the partial equilibrium Cournot–Nash model of imperfect competition, there is usually strategic substitutability across sellers of identical products. As other sellers produce more, the residual demand curve facing a single seller will shift in, thus inducing that agent to produce less. In addition, the economy exhibits a form of strategic complementarity across sectors.[2] The complementarity in this economy arises through income effects: expansions in the level of activity by producers in all other sectors increase the demand for products in the remaining sector and thus create an incentive for output expansion. The link across sectors is thus created by a relationship between current income and current expenditures.

Because of the presence of strategic substitutability in the quantity decisions of agents within a given sector, the model does not exactly correspond to the Cooper–John formulation or even to the more general structure described in the previous chapter. Nonetheless, the essential implications of strategic complementarities are preserved in this framework. Loosely speaking, the strategic substitutability across agents in a given sector is dominated by the interactions across the sectors.

---

2. An alternative model using monopolistic competition, as summarized in Blanchard–Kiyotaki [1987], can generate many of these same aggregate demand externalities. This approach is discussed later in this chapter.

Basic Structure

For simplicity, suppose that there are two sectors in the economy with F producers within a sector. For now we take F as given. There is also a nonproduced good. All agents have an endowment of $\bar{m}$ units of this good. Sector i agents have preferences given by

$$c_{-i}^{\alpha}m^{1-\alpha} - kq_i \tag{1}$$

So, a sector i producer consumes the good produced in the other sector and the nonproduced good. The disutility of production is given by kq_i, where q_i is the output of good i and $k < 1$. Note that we do not index producers since, in equilibrium, they will act identically. Of course, in characterizing the Nash equilibrium, we allow sellers to choose different output levels. The assumption that agents do not consume any of their own output is not important, but the fact that they consume the output of others is crucial: without this assumption there is no trade and thus no scope for coordination failures.

As buyers, agents take their income and consume the goods produced in other sectors. In this decision, they act as price takers. This is meant to capture the idea, formalized in Hart [1982], that agents are large in their own output sector but, in the presence of many sectors, are small in the overall economy.

With these simple preferences, a share α of total income (revenues plus the endowment of the nonproduced good) is spent on the good produced in the other sector and the remainder of income is used to purchase the nonproduced good. That is, demands are given by

$$c_{-i} = \alpha I_i/p_{-i} \quad \text{and} \quad m = (1 - \alpha)I_i$$

where I_i denotes the income of agent i. Utility is directly expressed over production (q_i) as

$$z(p_{-i})I_i - kq_i \tag{2}$$

where $z(p_{-i}) = (\alpha/p_{-i})^{\alpha}(1 - \alpha)^{(1-\alpha)}$ and I_i equals the revenues from production, p_iq_i, and the value of the endowment, $\bar{m}$, which is also the numeraire commodity. The function $z(p_{-i})$ is the utility per unit of numeraire.

A producer of good i will choose q_i to maximize indirect utility taking the output levels of other firms within the sector as given. Further, the producer takes as given the overall level of spending on the sector. Both of these influences are implicit in the sectoral price, p_i. This leads to the usual first-order condition equating marginal revenue and marginal cost,

$$p_i z(p_{-i})[1 + (q_i/p_i)\partial p_i/\partial q_i] = k \qquad (3)$$

Note that the optimization problem of the producer reflects both strategic and market interactions. The game arises between sellers of an identical product, in the traditional Cournot–Nash fashion. However, once quantities are determined, there is an auctioneer that appears to clear the markets for each of the goods. Of course, the producers anticipate the price the auctioneer will set to clear markets in making their individual quantity decisions. See Jones and Manuelli [1992] and Roberts [1987] for analyses of games of imperfect competition where prices and quantities are set strategically.

Equilibrium Conditions

The price of sector i goods satisfies market clearing: i.e., $p_i = E_i/Q_i$ where E_i is total spending on sector i and Q_i is the total output of good i. From the optimization problem for sector $-i$ agents, we know that $E_i = \alpha(p_{-i}Q_{-i} + F\bar{m})$. That is, a share α of the total income of agents in section $-i$ is spent on the goods produced by sector i agents.

Given that producers within a sector are identical, it is natural to focus on symmetric Nash equilibria within a sector. Let q_i be the output of good i per firm in sector i. Further, define $\eta \equiv (1 - (1/F))$. Here η conveniently summarizes the extent of imperfect competition in this market. As F gets large, η tends to 1, while, in the case of a monopolist, $\eta = 0$.

Using the first-order condition for profit maximization given by (3) and the condition for market clearing, in a symmetric Nash equilibrium the price of sector i must satisfy

$$p_i z(p_{-i})\eta = k \qquad (4)$$

Note that as a result of constant returns to scale and the assumed preferences, there are no quantities in (4).

Since the economy is also symmetric across sectors, the equilibrium price for sector $-i$ satisfies the analogue of (4). In a symmetric equilibrium $p_i = p^*$ for $i = 1, 2$ where, from (4), $(p^*)^{1-\alpha} = k/\mu\eta$, with $\mu \equiv \alpha^\alpha(1 - \alpha)^{1-\alpha}$.

Using this price in the market clearing condition implies that per firm output in sector i satisfies

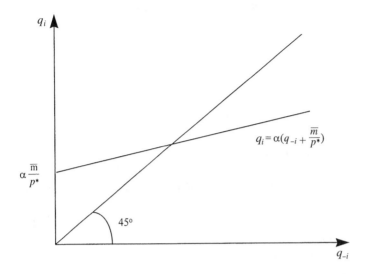

Figure 4.1

$$q_i = \alpha[q_{-i} + \overline{m}/p^*] \tag{5}$$

for $i = 1, 2$. The two equations given by (5) jointly determine the levels of output in both sectors. They provide the link to the strategic complementarity model since "reaction curves," linking the output per firm in sector i with that in sector $-i$, are upward sloping. That is, expansions in one sector create an incentive for producers in the other sector to expand as well. They also bear a striking resemblance to the simple income–expenditure model of Keynesian economics.[3]

Figure 4.1 illustrates the relationship between sectoral output levels from (5). If sector $-i$ output is zero, the demand per firm for good i is generated from the endowment of the nonproduced good to agents in the other sector, $\alpha \overline{m}/p^*$. This represents the "autonomous" level of expenditure on good i. Expansions of output per firm in sector $-i$ then increase demand for good i by α unit. This is the complementarity across sectors generated by final demand linkages.[4]

---

3. Note that prices are determined independently of quantities because of the assumption of a linear disutility of effort.
4. In some sense, there is nothing strategic per se about this linkage: it simply reflects the normality of goods in the producers' utility functions.

The symmetric Nash equilibrium for this economy is the level of output per firm in each sector, q^*, where

$$q^* = \frac{(\alpha \bar{m}/p^*)}{(1 - \alpha)} \tag{6}$$

Note that the level of output in this economy is unique. Given the linearity of the "reaction curve" there will be a single crossing with the 45° line. As noted later, the uniqueness reflects a variety of restrictions we have placed on the technology and preferences.

As one would expect, the level of output lies below the competitive solution. If firms had no market power at all, then $\eta = 1$ and $p^* = (k/\mu)^{1/(1-\alpha)}$. Since the price is a decreasing function of η, as the economy becomes more competitive, the symmetric equilibrium price falls and, from (6), the level of production increases.

In terms of welfare, the equilibrium level of utility for a producer in one of the sectors is

$$q^{*\alpha}\bar{m}^{(1-\alpha)} - kq^* \tag{7}$$

The derivative of this function with respect to q is given by

$$\alpha\left(\frac{m}{q^*}\right)^{(1-\alpha)} - k \tag{8}$$

Using the condition for the equilibrium level of output, this derivative can be rewritten as

$$\mu p^{(1-\alpha)} - k \tag{9}$$

From the equilibrium conditions, we know that $\mu p^{*(1-\alpha)}$ exceeds k since $\eta < 1$. Hence, as the economy becomes more competitive, q^* and welfare increase.

This is an interesting result because there are two effects present as the economy becomes more competitive. First, there is a congestion effect within a sector which decreases payoffs since a firm has more competitors. On the basis of this effect alone, an increase in the number of firms in any sector reduces the payoffs to those firms because of the increased competitiveness. Second, there is a positive externality associated with greater competition in the other sector of the economy: as consumers, agents face lower markups as the number of sellers in the other sector increases. The fact that welfare increases with the number of firms implies that the second effect is stronger than the first.[5]

The Multiplier

There is a multiplier in this economy stemming from changes in the level of real autonomous expenditure $(\overline{m}/p^*)$ on a given sector equal to $1/(1 - \alpha) > 1$. The magnitude of this multiplier depends, of course, on the strength of the demand linkage (measured by α) across the two sectors of the economy. Increases in autonomous expenditure by sector $-i$ shift out the demand for good i and induce sector i firms to expand output. This creates additional demand for sector $-i$ firms and thus additional revenues to be spent on sector i. These income–expenditure linkages form the basis of the multiplier.

These multiplier effects are extreme as a result of the assumption of constant marginal costs. Without that assumption, variations in the endowment of the nonproduced good would create fluctuations in the relative prices and quantities produced of the two goods. The relative magnitude of the price and quantity movements would then reflect the curvature of the function characterizing the disutility of work for an individual producer.

To what extent do these multiplier effects require imperfect competition? It is entirely possible that a perfectly competitive economy could have an equilibrium on a flat part of the marginal cost curve. In that case, the comparative static effects of an increase in the endowment of the nonproduced good could arise as well. Thus, the key to the multiplier in this economy is the slope of the marginal cost curve and not imperfect competition per se. Imperfect competition creates a markup of price over cost and thus reduces the level of employment. If marginal cost is convex, then production occurs at a flatter part of the marginal cost schedule, thus making multiplier effects more likely. This is particularly true if the economy has flat marginal cost to a capacity and the presence of market power is to move the economy from operating along the vertical part to the horizontal part of the marginal cost curve.

An importance difference between this model and that explored in Hart

---

5. Chatterjee–Cooper [1988] and Chatterjee–Cooper–Ravikumar [1993] use this property to develop models of multiple equilibria through the endogenous determination of the number of firms in each sector. If agents must incur a cost of participating in imperfectly competitive markets and this cost differs across the agents, there may exist thick (thin) market equilibria with high (low) levels of participation.

[1982] concerns labor markets and thus the possibility of underemployment. Hart assumes that labor markets are imperfectly competitive because of the presence of labor unions of syndicates. These groups of workers have market power while firms act competitively in the labor market. Further, Hart simplifies the analysis by assuming that workers have no disutility of work. Still, because of the market power on the supply side of the labor market, he is able to obtain underemployment equilibria and a multiplier.

Multiple Equilibria

Another aspect of these models is that the presence of imperfect competition creates the possibility of multiple, Pareto-ranked equilibria and thus coordination failures. This is, of course, not possible in a competitive environment, in which the First Fundamental Welfare Theorem holds. The example given did not have multiple equilibrium because of two important properties: the constant elasticity of demand and the linearity of the production process.

Heller [1986] provides an example of multiple equilibria based on variations in the elasticity of residual demand. The idea here is that for some reasonable preference structures the elasticity of demand will be relatively high at low levels of consumption and relatively low at higher levels of consumption. Combined with imperfect competition, this implies that markups will be relatively high (low) when output and consumption are low (high).

Alternatively, multiplicity can arise from nonconvexities in the production process. Consider a version of this multisector economy in which all firms in sector 1 choose output and the method of production. The former is a continuous choice, as earlier, while the latter is naturally discrete.

As in Cooper [1994], suppose that each firm can choose between two technologies. Technology j has a fixed cost of operation denoted by K_j and an associated marginal product of labor, θ_j, for $j = L, H$. Assume that $\theta_H > \theta_L$ and that $K_H > K_L$ so that technology H is more productive than technology L but also has a higher fixed cost of operation.

Which technique will a firm use? If sales are sufficiently high, then a firm should be willing to incur a high fixed cost to utilize the more productive technique. Alternatively, if demand and sales are low, then it may be more profitable for firms to use the less efficient technique to reduce overhead costs of production. One interesting example of this might be the choice between single and multishift production, assuming that starting a shift entails some fixed expenditures.

Of course, in an equilibrium model, sales are not exogenous but rather result from the activities of others. In the two-sector model, the output of sector 1 firms is sold to sector 2 producers, who, in turn, earn income from the production and sale of their own output. This sets the stage for multiple equilibria through the choice of technique by sector 1 firms.

Cooper [1994] proves that if α is sufficiently close to 1, so that the linkages across the sectors are strong, then multiple equilibria can arise. In one equilibrium, all of the sector 1 firms use the more productive technology. This is individually optimal since the choice of this technique by all firms leads to a lower sector 1 price, higher output from sector 2 firms and hence a lower sector 2 price as well. This lower price for sector 2 goods provides the inducement for the adoption of the high fixed cost technique by a representative sector 1 firm. In the second equilibrium, firms adopt the low fixed cost, low productivity technique, leading to high prices and relatively low levels of activity, which rationalize this equilibrium.

Cooper uses this model to argue that in the face of "demand shocks," modeled as variations in the endowment of the nonproduced good, productivity and output will be positively correlated as a result of variations in the choice of technique. The procyclical productivity is not the result of new inventions but rather the endogenous utilization decision of existing techniques.

MONOPOLISTIC COMPETITION

An alternative model of imperfect competition, also used widely in macroeconomics, assumes monopolistic competition. Here the conception is that each agent supplies a unique good to the market, so that, in contrast to the model described, there is no competition between producers of an identical product. Under the maintained assumption of a large number of products, the individual producer of a good (either a final good, an intermediate good or even a distinct form of labor service) takes the state of the aggregate economy as given when optimizing, though, as usual, the aggregate state does matter for the individual. This limited form of interaction simplifies the analysis greatly. As we shall see in the next section of this chapter, this model also facilitates a study of price setting behavior.

The model we analyze here is a simple extension of that explored in the previous section. Other versions of this model abound in the literature: Blanchard and Kiyotaki [1987] provides a rather thorough analysis of a general version of the economy including market power in both goods and labor markets.

Consider an economy in which there are J agents producing distinct goods. Let $j = 1, \ldots, J$ index the good and let i represent an arbitrary agent. As earlier, each agent is endowed with $\overline{m}$ units of a numeraire (nonproduced good) and some leisure time. In the monopolistic economy, each good j is produced by a unique agent and each agent produces a unique good. Preferences are given by

$$c_i^{\alpha} m_i^{1-\alpha} - kq_i \tag{10}$$

where c_i is an index of consumption, m_i is the consumption of the nonproduced good and k is a parameter describing the disutility of work. The production technology is quite simple: output (q_i) equals labor input.

The difference between this model and the one above concerns the index of consumption. Let the consumption index for agent i, c_i, be given by

$$c_i = \left(\sum_{j=1}^{j=J} c_{ij}^{(\theta-1)/\theta} \right)^{\theta/(\theta-1)} \tag{11}$$

where $\theta > 1$ parameterizes the degree of substitutability between goods in this CES specification. Note that an alternative, but equivalent formulation would treat the consumption aggregate as the output of a competitive production section, and the individual consumption goods would then be inputs into the production of the final good.

Each individual producer maximizes utility subject to a budget constraint:

$$\sum_{j=1}^{j=J} p_j c_{ij} + m_i = p_i n_i + \overline{m} = I_i \tag{12}$$

Here we use c_{ij} to denote the consumption of good j by agent i. Further, m_i is the consumption of the nonproduced good by that agent. Further, let I_i denote the income of agent i, which is composed of revenues from production and the endowment $\overline{m}$ of the nonproduced good.

To ease the analysis, it is convenient first to represent the demand functions for a representative agent and then to investigate the output choice of a representative producer. Given income I_i, agent i chooses a consumption bundle taking prices as given. In this way, the agent takes prices as given when acting as a consumer. The resulting demand functions for agent i are given by

$$m_i = (1-\alpha)I_i \quad \text{and} \quad c_{ij} = (\alpha I_i/P)(p_j/P)^{-\theta} \tag{13}$$

where P is the CES price index given by

$$P = \left((1/J)\sum_{j=1}^{j=J} p_j^{1-\theta}\right)^{1/(1-\theta)} \tag{14}$$

These demand functions have the usual property of Cobb–Douglas utility that the budget shares are given by $(1 - \alpha)$ for the nonproduced good and by α for the consumption index, i.e., $Pc_i = \alpha I_i$.

Using the demand function for the produced good by a representative agent, the aggregate demand for product j is

$$D_j = \frac{\alpha I}{P}(p_j/P)^{-\theta} \tag{15}$$

where I measures total income. As in the model of imperfect competition explored in the previous section, part of the interaction across agents will be determined, in equilibrium, by I. Our assumption that $\theta > 1$ implies that an increase in P will lead to an increase in the demand for product j given I and p_j. The increase in the aggregate price level reduces the real value of income but also creates a substitution effect which dominates the income effect.

We can now use D_j to determine the optimal output level of an individual producer taking *both* P and I as given. Using the fact that both c_i and m_i are proportional to I_i, the individual producer maximizes

$$\mu P^{-\alpha}[p_i n_i + M] - kn_i \tag{16}$$

where μ is again a constant function of α as in the previous section. The demand function for good i, from (15), is used in this optimization problem. The first-order condition will generally express the relationship between the price of product i, optimally set by the choice of output by producer i, as a function of aggregate income (I) and the price level P. However, with constant marginal costs and the constant elasticity of demand implied by the CES preference structure, the first-order condition is independent of the output level and is simply

$$p_i = kP^{\alpha}/[(1 - (1/\theta))\mu] \tag{17}$$

Thus the optimal price for an individual is an increasing function of the aggregate price level since α is positive. Further, the markup of price over marginal cost (k) is proportional to $(1 - 1/\theta)$ so that large markups are associated with low values of θ. This makes good economic sense. If goods are not highly substitutable, then the producer has more market power, which is reflected in a larger markup.

The equilibrium of the model is characterized by a vector of prices and output levels for each product such that individuals are optimizing and all markets clear. As in numerous examples already seen in this book, the natural output is a symmetric equilibrium in which $p = P = P^*$. The market clearing price P^* is given by

$$P^* = \left(\frac{k}{\mu(1 - (1/\theta))}\right)^{(1/(1-\alpha))} \tag{18}$$

Note that this is essentially the same equilibrium price as that given for the multisector model of imperfect competition.

At these prices, the equilibrium output of a given sector, denoted by y^*, is determined from demand. Since all prices are set at P^* and all agents produce at the same level, total income in the economy must be $J[P^*y^*] + M$ so that

$$y^* = \alpha[y^* + M/P^*] = \frac{\alpha(M/P^*)}{1 - \alpha} \tag{19}$$

where M is the aggregate endowment of the nonproduced good in the economy.

The output effect of the monopolistic competition is to raise the equilibrium price level and thus to lower the equilibrium output. Perfect competition here occurs when products are perfectly substitutable so that $\theta \to \infty$. In this case, P^* and output go to their competitive levels.

It is interesting to compare (18) and (19) with the Nash equilibrium of the imperfectly competitive economy given by (4) and (6). Since both the economy with quantity setting Cournot–Nash firms and the monopolistic competition economy specified here assume constant marginal cost, it is not very surprising that equilibrium prices can be determined independently of the level of output. Note, though, that this property also rests on the assumptions regarding preferences such that demand elasticities are constant. Further, the two output expressions are identical: in both cases output is proportional to the real value of the stock of the nonproduced good. In both cases, this outside good provides a basis for the expenditures of the economy and, also, through the Cobb–Douglas preferences, provides a leakage out of the expenditure stream.

One important difference between the two economies is the source of market power. For the multisector Cournot–Nash model, market power is created by the assumption of a small number of sellers of each particular product. The degree of market power is thus parameterized by the number of firms. In contrast, the key parameter for the model of monopolistic competition is the degree of substitutability between products.

MONEY AND MENU COSTS

There are additional contributions of imperfect competition models. One of them concerns the price setting behavior of firms when prices are costly to adjust. Ball and Romer [1990] consider the set of Nash equilibria in a price setting game between monopolistic competitors. As in the related work of Blanchard and Kiyotaki [1987] and as discussed in the previous section, the preferences are structured so that the best response of price setter *i* to an increase in the aggregate price level is to increase his own price as well. That is, these models of monopolistic competition have a strategic complementarity in prices. If one then embeds this price setting game into an aggregate model with changes in both the money supply and menu costs, Ball and Romer show that multiple equilibria, in terms of the response of prices to the stock of money, may arise. In one equilibrium, prices are flexible, and in another, as a result of the menu cost, no agent, acting alone, wishes to change prices given that others are not changing their prices. The point is simply that the gains to changing prices are higher if others change them as well.

Of course, the model presented earlier must be amended to accommodate an analysis of monetary shocks since the basic model of monopolistic competition does not contain money. It is tempting to treat the nonproduced good as money, but care must be taken to understand the demand for money and the basis for its nonneutrality. In terms of money demand, these extensions of the models of monopolistic competition take the simple but direct approach of putting money into the utility function. This has the desired effect of creating a demand for money, though the source of this demand is not made clear. One possibility would be to extend the analysis to, say, a two-period overlapping generations model so that money is held as a store of value.

With regard to the issue of money nonneutrality, the point of the analysis is to create real effects of money based upon costs of adjusting prices. One of the themes in this literature is that a small menu cost can create "large" welfare effects in the presence of a distortion such as market power. On this point, the standard reference is Mankiw [1985].

To see this somewhat more formally, we consider a fairly general model of price setting behavior and then specialize it to understand the results of Ball and Romer. The starting point of the analysis is the profit function of a monopolistic competitor, as in the model of the previous section.

We denote the current profit flow by $W(M/P, p/P)$ where P is a measure of aggregate prices, M is the stock of fiat money and p is the current price of the seller. Think of M as a stochastic variable, reflecting the policies of the monetary authority. P is again a summary statistic for the decisions of other sellers in the economy and is viewed as outside the control of the individual seller. Thus M/P is an exogenous random variable from the perspective of the individual seller. In contrast, the seller has an influence on his relative price, p/P.

The profit function $W(M/P, p/P)$ can be derived from the model of monopolistic competition given earlier, recognizing that M/P, a measure of aggregate expenditures, and p/P, the relative price, are the two arguments in the demand curve facing an individual producer. Thus utility can be written as a function of these two variables. Ball and Romer provide more details on this point, and for now we can view this profit function as a primitive object.

Assume that in each period, the seller can either leave his price at p or change it. For simplicity, we assume that these changes take effect immediately, though the seller bears a fixed cost of price adjustment (a menu cost) of F. Using the state vector $s = (M/P, p/P)$, the optimization problem of a seller can conveniently be expressed as a dynamic programming problem where $V(s)$ is the value function defined over the current state:

$$V(s) = \max\ [W(M/P, p/P) + \beta EV(M'/P', p/P'), \qquad (20)$$
$$\max_{p*} W(M/P, p*/P) - F + \beta EV(M'/P', p*/P')]$$

So, in the first term, the seller doesn't change his price and thus sells goods at a relative price of p/P today. The stochastic evolution of M and P is reflected in the expectation of the future value of being in state s'.

For the second option, the seller incurs a cost of F to change the price of some other, denoted by p^*. Note that the optimization problem that yields p^* takes into account both the current and future effects of having this new price. Further, as in the model described in the previous section, the seller views P as independent of his action.

The qualitative properties of the solution to the single agent problem is not difficult to understand.[6] The agent will adopt a strategy of inaction as long as p/P is not too far from its optimal point given M/P. Once p/P is outside the inaction set, then the agent will act.

Of course, the equilibrium analysis must go beyond this point since we are interested in more than the optimization problem of a single agent. To analyze the equilibrium we note that the variable P, while exogenous to the single agent, reflects the joint decisions of all agents. Thus the characterization of the state dependent equilibrium requires the solution of the individual dynamic optimization problem and a fixed point type argument to ensure the consistency of P with the individual state dependent decisions.

Ball and Romer do not tackle this very difficult problem but instead simplify it by considering an essentially static framework.[7] Their analysis succeeds in bringing to light the possibility of multiple equilibria in this and related environments. Suppose that in the previous period price changes had occurred so that the economy was in an equilibrium in which all agents charged the same price: $p = P$. Further, assume that M stock of fiat money is such that $M/P = 1$. This is the equilibrium of the economy in the event that $F = 0$ and thus provides a useful initial condition.

Given this, a new value of M is randomly drawn. Price setters must decide whether to change their price or not and do so to maximize static profits alone. Thus, Ball and Romer essentially ignore the future effects of changing prices today.

First, we consider the conditions such that sellers do not change their prices. Given that all others keep their price fixed at P, a given seller will do so as well as long as

$$W(M, 1) \geq W(M, p^*/P) - F \tag{21}$$

6. Important references include Caballero–Engel [1993], Caplin–Leahy [1991, 1997], and Dotsey, King and Wolman [1996]. One interesting aspect of these papers is the connection between the magnitude of strategic complementarity and the nature of output and price fluctuations in response to monetary shocks.
7. Caplin–Leahy [1997] finds the general equilibrium of a related economy without the emphasis of Ball–Romer on multiplicity.

Here $W(M/P, p^*/P)$ denotes the current period payoff from selecting p^* given the aggregate price level and the nominal money supply. According to Ball and Romer, a second-order Taylor expansion of this around the initial equilibrium point of $(1, 1)$ implies that there exists an equilibrium with price rigidity for values of M in the interval $(1 - x^*, 1 + x^*)$. Put differently, for values of M further away from 1 than x^*, even if others keep their price fixed, the representative seller will vary his price. In their analysis,

$$x^* = \sqrt{\frac{-2W_{22}F}{(W_{12})^2}} \tag{22}$$

where W_{12} and W_{22} are the derivatives of the profit function evaluated at $(1, 1)$.

Alternatively, suppose that all others adjust prices to p^{**}, the equilibrium price given adjustment. Thus the aggregate price level is $P^{**} = p^{**}$ in the face of the money supply change. This is an equilibrium as long as

$$W(M/P^{**}, 1) - F \geq W(M/P^{**}, p/P^{**}) \tag{23}$$

where p represents the initial price of the representative seller. By not adjusting, the seller incurs a relative price change but avoids the menu cost. For this case, there is also a maximal absolute value change in M, call it x^{**}, such that adjustment is an equilibrium if M lies *outside* the internal $(1 - x^{**}, 1 + x^{**})$.

The issue of multiplicity is determined by the relative sizes of x^* and x^{**}. If $x^{**} < x^*$, then there exists a region of values of M such that agents will change prices if others do but will keep their prices fixed if others do not change theirs. Ball and Romer find that $x^*/x^{**} = 1/\pi$ where $\pi \equiv -W_{12}/W_{22}$. Assuming that profits are strictly concave in the price level of a seller, i.e., $W_{22} < 0$, the sign of π is determined by the sign of W_{12}. In fact, π is equivalent to the derivative of the optimal relative price of seller i (p_i/P) with respect to the aggregate level of real spending (M/P).

For $x^{**} < x^*$, it must be the case that $\pi < 1$. With this model, this is equivalent to the condition that the reaction function, expressing the optimal price of a seller as a function of the aggregate price, is increasing and crosses the 45° line with a slope less than 1. That is,

$$dp_i/dP = \frac{W_{12} + W_{22}}{W_{22}} = 1 - \pi \tag{24}$$

So, the condition of strategic complementarity in the price setting process along with a stability condition implies that there are multiple equilibria in the static version of the price setting game. This is an interesting result, though questions about its robustness to a more dynamic setting remain open to discussion.

QUANTITATIVE EVIDENCE ON DYNAMIC MODELS OF IMPERFECT COMPETITION

The final point of this chapter is to make note of efforts to undertake a quantitative analysis of the aggregate economy from the perspective of a model with monopolistic competition. A useful starting point is the analysis of Chatterjee and Cooper [1993], who investigate the basic model of monopolistic competition in the stochastic growth model with capital accumulation.[8] The Chatterjee–Cooper model allows for the endogenous determination of the number of products and thus extends the prior model of Hornstein [1993]. In fact, the presentation of the Chatterjee–Cooper model provides a vehicle for understanding the results of Hornstein as well.

Household and Firm Optimization

This section describes the decision problems for the many firms and the single representative consumer of the economy. As in the basic model of monopolistic competition, each of the firms produces a different good. In contrast, for this economy that good can be either consumed directly or used to produce an investment good which becomes capital in the future. Thus there are two CES functions, which, respectively, describe the production of composite consumption and investment goods from the specific commodities. Further, for this economy, the number of products is endogenous.

Let N_t denote the number of producing firms (equivalently, products) in period t with p_{ct}^j and p_{it}^j as the consumption and investment price of the jth good, $j \in \{1, 2, \ldots N_t\}$. The consumer derives utility from leisure and the consumption of each of the produced goods and earns income from renting labor and capital to firms and also receives the profits of the firms.

---

8. Thus this discussion draws heavily upon this paper with Satyajit Chatterjee.

The wage rate is denoted w_t and the rental price of a unit of capital is q_t. The optimization problem for a representative consumer is given by

$$\max \sum_{t=0}^{\infty} \beta^t u(c_t, l_t)$$

$$\text{s.t.} \sum_{j=1}^{N_t} p_{ct}^j c_t^j + \sum_{j=1}^{N_t} p_{it}^j i_t^j \le w_t(1-l_t) + q_t k_t + \sum_{j=1}^{N_t} \pi_t^j$$

$$k_{t+1} = (1-\delta)k_t + i_t \tag{25}$$

$$c_t = \left(\sum_{j=1}^{N_t} c_t^{j^{1/v}} \right)^v, \quad i_t = \left(\sum_{j=1}^{N_t} i_t^{j^{1/\theta}} \right)^\theta, \quad v > 1, \quad \theta > 1$$

$$c_t \ge 0, \quad i_t^j \ge 0, \quad 1 \ge l_t \ge 0$$

Note that the consumption of each of the goods produced enters the utility function through a symmetric CES aggregator with elasticity of substitution given by $v/(1 - v)$. Similarly, as in Kiyotaki [1988], investment in period t is a symmetric CES aggregate with elasticity of substitution $(\theta/(1 - \theta))$. The use of these two separate aggregators is meant to capture the importance of diversity for consumers as well as producers without straying too far from the traditional one-sector model. This specification allows us to capture imperfect substitutability within consumer goods as distinct from the degree of substitutability of inputs into the investment process. From the consumer's side, the CES function represents a home production function in which consumption goods purchased in period t are used to produce a consumption aggregate, c_t. Similarly, the consumer purchases a variety of investment goods which are combined to produce additional capital in the following period.

Given c_t and i_t, the consumption and investment demand for good j in period t is given by

$$c_t^j = c_t \left(\frac{p_{ct}^j}{p_{ct}} \right)^{\frac{v}{1-v}}, \quad i_t^j = i_t \left(\frac{p_{it}^j}{p_{it}} \right)^{\frac{\theta}{1-\theta}} \tag{26}$$

where p_{ct} and p_{it} are price indices given by

$$P_{ct} = \left(\sum_{j=1}^{N_t} (p_{ct}^j)^{\frac{1}{1-v}} \right)^{1-v}, \quad p_{it} = \left(\sum_{j=1}^{N_t} (p_{it}^j)^{\frac{1}{1-\theta}} \right)^{1-\theta} \tag{27}$$

These conditions for consumer demand, given c_t, are essentially identical to those generated by the static economy. The intertemporal optimization is, of course, reflected in the allocation of current income between consumption and investment.

These price indices show the benefit of variety effects: if the price of all types of consumption (investment) goods is the same, then, since v and θ exceed 1, the consumption (investment) price index is a decreasing function of N_t. Therefore, an increase in the number of products lowers the cost of consumption and investment relative to leisure. If $v \neq \theta$, an increase in N_t also alters the cost of the consumption good relative to the investment good; in particular, it falls if $v < \theta$. Intuitively, these effects arise because the produced goods are imperfect substitutes for each other. As more of them become available it becomes easier (i.e., cheaper) to satisfy a given level of demand. Note that the strength of these effects depends on the degree to which v or θ departs from 1; the number of firms has no effect on the price indices when v and θ are 1: i.e., the goods are perfect substitutes for each other.

Using the price indices noted in (27), the budget constraint in the consumer's problem can be compactly written as

$$p_{ct}c_t + p_{it}i_t \leq w_t(1-l_t) + q_t k_t + \sum_{j=1}^{N_t} \pi_t^j \tag{28}$$

Thus, ignoring nonnegativity constraints, the intratemporal and intertemporal efficiency conditions are

$$\frac{u_l(c_t,\ l_t)}{u_c(c_t,\ l_t)} = \frac{w_t}{p_{ct}} \tag{29}$$

$$u_c(c_t,\ l_t)\left(\frac{p_{it}}{p_{ct}}\right) = \beta u_c(c_{t+1},\ l_{t+1})\left(\frac{q_{t+1}}{p_{ct+1}} + (1-\delta)\frac{p_{it+1}}{p_{ct+1}}\right) \tag{30}$$

From the Euler equation, given by (30), the consumer's loss from reducing the consumption index by a unit in period t, purchasing some of the investment index, equals the gain obtained by consuming the proceeds from first renting the capital and then selling the undepreciated capital in the following period.

Each of the N_t firms active in the economy in period t produces a single, unique good. Good j, produced by seller j, can be sold to consumers either as a consumption good (at a price p_{ct}^j) or as an investment good (at a price p_{it}^j). Thus, we assume that the firm can price discriminate between consumption and investment goods markets.

Since the capital accumulation decision is made by the consumer, each firm needs to solve a static profit maximization problem. Each firm takes factor prices as given but recognizes its market power in the commodity market. The production function $F(...)$, given more explicitly later, is characterized by overhead labor $(\bar{n})$ and overhead capital $(\bar{k})$. The overhead costs are important as they allow the existence of market power with no excessive profits on average. Variations in the technology parameter, A_t, will be a source of fluctuations in the economy.

Equilibrium Analysis

Since the output of each active firm appears symmetrically in the consumption and investment aggregate, the equilibrium quantity and price of each good will be the same. An equilibrium is then a sequence of consumption, output, employment, investment and prices such that individuals optimize, markets clear and firms earn zero profits (reflecting free entry).

As shown in Chatterjee and Cooper, the conditions for consumer and firm optimization can be used to eliminate the price, wage and capital-rental terms. Therefore, the conditions of equilibrium reduce to the following equations:

$$\frac{u_l(c_t, 1 - n_t)}{u_c(c_t, 1 - n_t)} = A_t N_t^{\gamma-1} \frac{F_n(n_t - N_t\bar{n}, k_t - N_t\bar{k})}{\nu} \tag{31}$$

$$u_c(c_t, 1 - n_t)\frac{\theta}{\nu}N_t^{\gamma-\theta} = \beta u_c(c_{t+1}, 1 - n_{t+1}) \tag{32}$$

$$\left\{ A_{t+1}N_{t+1}^{\gamma-1}\frac{F_k(n_{t+1} - N_{t+1}\bar{n}, k_{t+1} - N_{t+1}\bar{k})}{\nu} + (1 - \delta)\frac{\theta}{\nu}N_{t+1}^{\gamma-\theta} \right\}$$

$$c_t + N_t^{\gamma-\theta}\{k_{t+1} - (1 - \delta)k_t\} = A_t N_t^{\gamma-1}F(n_t - N_t\bar{n}, k_t - N_t\bar{k}) \tag{33}$$

$$c_t + \frac{\theta}{\nu}N_t^{\gamma-\theta}\{k_{t+1} - (1 - \delta)k_t\} \tag{34}$$

$$= A_t N_t^{\gamma-1}\left\{ \frac{F_n(n_t - N_t\bar{n}, k_t - N_t\bar{k})}{\nu}n_t + \frac{F_n(n_t - N_t\bar{n}, k_t - N_t\bar{k})}{\nu}k_t \right\}$$

$$\lim_{t\to\infty}\beta^t u_c(c_t, n_t)k_{t+1} = 0 \tag{35}$$

The first two are the familiar intratemporal and intertemporal efficiency conditions. The third equation is the resource balance condition for the firm (i.e., the constraint in the optimization problem of the firm) expressed in terms of economywide variables. The fourth condition is the zero profit condition of firms, also expressed in terms of economywide variables. The final equation is the transversality condition.

Note that this system of equations nests two interesting models. One is the perfectly competitive neoclassical macroeconomic model analyzed in King, Plosser and Rebelo [1988]. This basic model corresponds to the case where $v = \theta = 1$ and $\bar{n} = \bar{k} = 0$. The second is the model explored by Hornstein where monopolistic competition is present but there is no entry or exit.

Relative to these other models, there are a couple of points worth noting. First, the total factor productivity term A_t in the basic model is replaced by the composite term $A_t N_t^{v-1}$ on the right hand side of (31)–(35). Since N_t is an endogenous variable, the effective total factor productivity in our model is endogenous and positively related to N_t since $v > 1$.

Intuitively, we would expect an increase in A_t to increase the equilibrium number of firms in period t so that a given exogenous shock to productivity would be larger in the imperfectly competitive model than in the competitive model: i.e., the imperfectly competitive model *magnifies* the impact of productivity disturbances.

An increase in total effective factor productivity in period t would also encourage more accumulation of capital, which in turn increases the number of firms in future periods. Therefore, even if the original shock to A_t is purely temporary, effective factor productivity will be serially correlated: i.e., the imperfectly competitive model provides additional *propagation* of productivity disturbances.

A second important aspect of introducing imperfect competition is that the presence of overhead labor and overhead capital influences the responsiveness of the economy to underlying shocks. As discussed in Hornstein [1993] as well, the key to understanding the effects of monopolistic competition (leaving aside product space variations through entry and exit) concerns the introduction of overhead costs, which are needed to absorb the profits from markups.

Following the approach of King, Plosser and Rebelo, Chatterjee and Cooper perform a quantitative analysis of their economy. Many aspects of the parameterization are from the basic neoclassical model. However, two key parameters for this study are θ and v: the degrees of substitution between consumption and investment goods. Chatterjee and Cooper look at two cases.

The first, termed *small markups,* follows Hornstein [1993] and sets $\theta = v = 1.5$ so that the markup of price over cost is 50%. This is a fairly conservative estimate of markups given the estimates reported in Hall [1988]. The ratio of production to nonproduction workers (a proxy for the overhead labor ratio) is set at .5, consistent with the evidence discussed in Davis and Haltiwanger [1991].[9]

The second, termed *large markups,* sets $\theta = \nu = 2$, closer to the upper range of Hall's estimates. For these higher values of markups, the overhead labor and capital ratios equal 1 so that labor's technology coefficient remains at .64.

Looking at the response to temporary technology shocks is useful since this provides evidence on the response to shocks and their propagation.[10] The model with perfect competition has many features that we normally associate with aggregate fluctuations: consumption is less volatile than output, investment is more volatile than output and there are positive contemporaneous correlations between key macroeconomic variables and output. However, as the technology shocks which drive the economy are transitory, there is little serial correlation in output fluctuations.

The addition of monopolistic competition *without* allowing for product space variation over the business cycle slightly increases the volatility of consumption and its correlation with output and somewhat reduces both the volatility of investment and its correlation with output. More importantly, employment fluctuations appear to be dampened by the introduction of monopolistic competition.

Since the analysis is conducted using an approximation around the steady state, one might think initially that adding in market power through markups would have little impact on the time series properties. However, this is not the case. By construction, the effects of monopolistic competition are not due to different estimates of parameters in the Cobb–Douglas technology. In fact, as explained earlier, the existence of markups implies the presence of overhead labor and capital, which dampens the response of firms to variations in the state of technology.

In the absence of entry, profits of firms are highly procyclical. The entry treatment allows potential entrants to respond to profit opportunities in their participation decisions. The propagation effects of the monopolistically competitive environment with entry and exit are evident from the fact that the serial correlation of output is .02, about four times that produced by the competitive economy. This increased serial correlation in output comes

---

9. This estimate of the overhead labor ratio has the virtue of implying that our estimate of the exponent on the labor input in our production function is the same as labor's income share. Note that we are calibrating the overhead capital and labor ratios and not the overhead capital and labor requirements directly.

10. Details of these calculations appear in Chatterjee–Cooper.

from the sources identified in our previous discussion: a temporary technology shock induces a product space expansion, which fosters more capital accumulation, and, in subsequent periods, the number of products remains above its steady state value. Still, at these low levels of the markup, there is relatively little internal propagation.

For the large markup treatment, there is substantially more endogenous propagation of the shocks. The amount of serial correlation in output from the transitory productivity shock is .13. There is also substantial serial correlation in consumption (.31), though none in either investment or employment.

SUMMARY

This chapter presented another class of economies in which complementarities were present. Here the departure from the Arrow–Debreu economy arises from the presence of market power.

Two basic models were presented. In the first, firms were large in a given market but small in the overall economy. For this economy, the interaction across firms within a market was characterized as strategic substitutability, while the interaction across sectors was one of strategic complementarity. Here we found the possibility of underemployment, multiple equilibria and multiplier effects. A second economy, one with monopolistic competition, was also developed. In fact, except for the source of market power, these two economies were analytically quite similar.

The monopolistically competitive economy was used to study two issues in macroeconomics. The first concerned the relevance of menu costs and money nonneutrality. Here we used a model from Ball and Romer to argue that in the presence of menu costs there may exist multiple equilibria in terms of the decisions of firms to change their prices.

The second exercise was to look at the quantitative properties of these models. Here we found that the model of monopolistic competition with entry and exit provided a vehicle for the magnification and propagation of temporary technology shocks. Further development of these models indicates that they can mimic many of the basic properties of U.S. data though determining the magnitude of markups, and their cyclical sensitivity is a continuing area of research.[11]

11. In a series of papers, Rotemberg and Woodford have also developed a theory of cyclical variations in markups using a supergame approach.

5   Thick Markets: Search and Matching

The next class of models stresses interactions between agents that reflect various forms of trading externalities. Here the linkages between agents do not arise directly in preferences or the production process but rather in the way agents come together to trade. Thus, these models rest firmly on the view that the Walrasian auctioneer does not function to bring together traders. Instead, trade frictions arise from the process of search and recruitment.

The complementarity in these models stems from the "thick market." This is essentially a restriction on the relationship between trading costs and the level of economic activity. In particular, the economies we explore have the property that if there are many agents in the market searching for trading partners, then the returns to participating in the market are higher as a result of reduced costs of search. Thus thick market effects are just the opposite of congestion effects: the thicker the market the lower are trading costs.

AN EXAMPLE

The flavor of these models can be seen through a simple example of a participation complementarity.[1] Denote by $Z(p)$ the return to an individual from participating in an activity if a proportion, p, of others are participat-

---

1. This example comes from Chatterjee–Cooper [1988] and is similar to one presented in Howitt [1991].

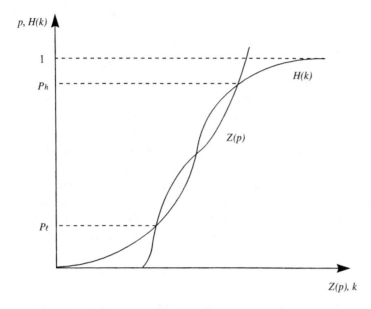

Figure 5.1

ing. *Assume* that $Z'(\cdot) > 0$ so that thicker markets are more desirable. The economics underlying this assumption will be the focus of the discussion to follow. Suppose that agent i's opportunity cost of participating is k_i and that these costs are distributed across the population with a cumulative distribution function given by $H(k)$, for $k \varepsilon [0, 1]$. Further, assume that $Z(0) > 0$ and $Z(1) < 1$. So, at zero participation, those with near 0 participation costs will choose to participate. Further, even if all others were participating, those with high opportunity costs would choose not to participate. These assumptions play the same role of guaranteeing an interior equilibrium as those made for the Cooper and John model developed earlier.

In a participation equilibrium, agent i takes p as given and participates if and only if $Z(p) \geq k_i$. That is, agent i will participate iff the gain to participation exceeds the cost.

An equilibrium is characterized by a critical participation rate, p^*, and a critical participation cost, k^*, such that $Z(p^*) = k^*$ and $p^* = H(k^*)$. In an equilibrium, if p^* agents participate, then all agents with $k_i \leq k^* \equiv Z(p^*)$ will participate. If $H(k^*) = p^*$, then the participation rate is self-fulfilling.

Figure 5.1 shows equilibria in this type of participation game. Here, the variable k is on the horizontal axis, while p is measured along the vertical axis. Thus the function $H(k)$ is plotted as a cumulative distribution function in the usual manner. The function $Z(p)$ maps from points along the vertical axis to values of k along the horizontal axis.

Since $Z(\cdot)$ and $H(\cdot)$ are independent, it is easy to construct examples of multiple participation equilibria. This is shown in the figure by the multiple crossings of the $Z(\cdot)$ and $H(\cdot)$ functions. As $Z'(\cdot) > 0$ by assumption, these equilibria will be Pareto-ranked by the level of market participation. Markets which are thick (p_h) are Pareto-preferred to thin $(p)_1$ markets because of the positive externality associated with $Z'(\cdot) > 0$.

The crucial assumption in this example is that $Z'(\cdot) > 0$. The contribution of the other papers in the participation complementarity literature is to provide interesting economic contexts in which this condition is met. In the work of Diamond [1982] and Howitt [1985], the returns to participation increase with p since thicker markets reduce transaction costs, in particular search costs. In Chatterjee and Cooper [1988] and Pagano [1989a, 1989b], the entry decisions of firms in imperfectly competitive markets generate a similar condition: agents would rather have market power as sellers in a thick market equilibrium than in one with thin markets. This may appear counterintuitive since firms with market power generally are better off as the number of competitors falls. In general equilibrium, that effect is present but, as argued in the previous subsection, is outweighed by the fact that firms (i.e., their owners) must spend the proceeds from sales on consumption goods and hence are affected by the market power of firms as consumers too. We now turn to the development of these models.

DIAMOND MODEL

To begin, we consider the model analyzed in Diamond [1982]. This model provides a simple framework to understand the notion of thick market complementarities. As in the example given, the key is that the returns to production are higher when many other agents are producing. This complementarity arises through the matching process of individual agents. This is also a useful model to study as it forms the basis of the Kiyotaki–Wright [1993] search model with money that we study later in this chapter.

We illustrate the model through the time-honored tradition of casting macroeconomics in terms of tropical islands. Suppose that individuals face a production decision: to climb a coconut tree and retrieve the fruit or pass up the opportunity. Trees are of varying heights so that agents optimally decide on a cutoff and climb trees iff they are shorter than the cutoff. If the agent elects to climb the tree, he must then meet a trading partner since, by assumption, agents do not consume the goods they produce. The likelihood of meeting another agent is assumed to be an increasing function of the number of agents looking to trade coconuts. This creates an underlying trading complementarity in the model: when markets are thick, trades are more likely. This is the basis of the multiple equilibria: if markets are thick (thin), then agents will optimally choose a high (low) cutoff, and, in a symmetric equilibrium, markets will be thick (thin) since there are many (few) traders searching for a partner.

To be more specific, consider an environment in which agents have production opportunities that have a stochastic cost $c \geq \hat{c}$ with a cumulative distribution function given by $G(c)$.[2] Time is continuous and these production opportunities arrive with probability α in each instant.[3] The arrival rate of production opportunities is exogenous and independent of the level of activity in the economy. Agents searching for a production opportunity are termed unemployed. Once a production chance is received, agents must decide to incur the production cost c or forgo the production opportunity. If production occurs, the cost is incurred instantaneously and a unit of output is produced.

Let e denote the proportion of agents (termed employed) with a unit of a good in storage in search of a trading partner. By assumption, this unit of output cannot be consumed by its producer so the agent must wait for the arrival of a trading partner. The agent is assumed to meet another agent with a unit of the good in storage with probability $b(e)$ in every instant of time, with $b(0) = 0$.

The key to this model, and the source of the trading complementarity, is that the probability of meeting a trading partner is an *increasing* function of the fraction of agents (e) in search of a trading partner. Diamond assumes that goods are indivisible so that once two agents meet, they simply swap the goods they each hold in inventory. Hence, thick markets (high values of e) imply that the instantaneous probability of meeting a trading partner is higher, thus increasing the returns to production. Thus,

2. $\hat{c} > 0$ places a lower bound on the costs of production.
3. Formally, the arrival of production activities is a Poisson process with an arrival rate of α.

one can see that the possibility of multiple equilibria, indexed by the level of trading activity, can emerge as a result of the presence of a strategic complementarity induced by the search process.

Let W^e be the lifetime return to an (employed) agent with a unit of the good to trade. Likewise, let W^u be the lifetime return to an (unemployed) agent awaiting the arrival of a production opportunity. Then,

$$rW^e = b(y - W^e + W^u) \tag{1}$$

and

$$rW^u = \alpha \int_0^{c^*} (W^e - W^u - c)dG(c) \tag{2}$$

In these expressions, note that a steady state assumption is being imposed since the value assigned to the states of employment and unemployment are not indexed by time. Expression (1) says that the flow of utility from employment equals the utility flow from consumption (y) plus the capital gain from switching to the unemployment state. This flow occurs with probability b. Likewise, (2) says that the flow from being unemployed is the cost of production plus the capital gain from switching to the employment state, which occurs with probability α. These two conditions can be derived from a discrete time model in which agents who meet a trading partner obtain a utility flow and switch to searching for a production opportunity with a one-period delay.

Implicit in the determination of W^u is a critical cost of production, c^*, that plays the role of k^* in the abstract participation complementarity problem described earlier. Individual optimality requires that at the critical production cost, the individual is just indifferent between producing or waiting for another production opportunity: i.e., $c^* = W^e - W^u$. Using this condition, (1) and (2) can be solved simultaneously to yield a relationship between c^* and the fraction of traders with inventory, i.e.,

$$c^* = \frac{b(e)y + \alpha \int_0^{c^*} cdG(c)}{r + b(e) + \alpha G(c^*)} \tag{3}$$

With $b'(\cdot) > 0$, this condition implies that the critical production cost is an increasing function of e. An increase in e implies that the returns to

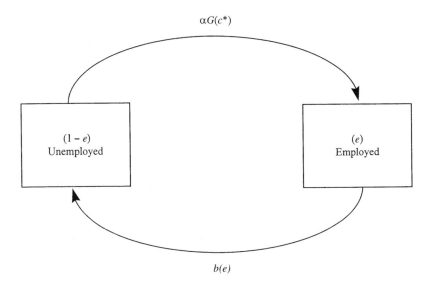

Figure 5.2

production are higher, rationalizing a larger c^*. A little bit of algebra shows that c^* is a concave function of e as long as $b''(\cdot) < 0$. Further, when $e = 0$, $c^* = 0$ as well since $b(0) = 0$.

This characterization of c^* provides the basis for the complementarity in the model. If all other agents in the economy select a high cutoff value, then e will be high and this rationalizes a high value of c^* for the remaining agent. The responsiveness of e to variations in c^* is governed by the cumulative distribution function, $G(\cdot)$.

In addition to these conditions describing the individual choices, there is an equation that describes the evolution of the e, the proportion of traders searching for a partner. As we follow Diamond and concentrate on steady states, the inflows and outflows from the employment state are equal, implying

$$\dot{e} = \alpha(1 - e)G(c^*) - eb(e) = 0 \tag{4}$$

The inflows into the employed group are given by the fraction of agents currently unemployed who find a production opportunity with a cost less than c^*, given by $\alpha(1 - e)G(c^*)$. The flow out of the employment group is the fraction of employed traders finding a trading partner, $eb(e)$. Figure 5.2 illustrates the flow of agents across states.

It is important to note that this condition implies a second positive relationship between c^* and e. An increase in c^* implies that more agents will be searching for trading partners. To offset this inflow into employment, more traders must be matched: hence e must rise to increase b. For $c^* \, \varepsilon \, [0, \hat{c}]$, (4) is satisfied at $e = 0$.

Thus we are left with two equations, (3) and (4), and two unknowns, c^* and e. The simultaneous solutions of these equations characterize the steady states for the model. They key issue is determining whether or not there are multiple equilibria for this economy.

As in the participation complementarity example, these two upward sloping curves can have multiple crossings. Hence, both thin and thick market equilibria may arise. The ease in generating multiple equilibria is partly due to the freedom in the model provided by the curvature of $G(\cdot)$, which is imbedded in the condition for a steady state level of e.

In Diamond's model, the multiple equilibria can be Pareto-ordered.[4] For an individual agent, an increase in e, given $c = c^*$, increases utility in both the employment (W^e) and unemployment (W^u) states. The fact that the individual then finds it optimal to increase c with e increases welfare further. Hence, the equilibria with thick markets will Pareto-dominate those with thin markets.

In equilibria with a low value of c^*, many production opportunities will be bypassed as they are "too costly" relative to the expected gains to trade. Trading opportunities are, in fact, bleak since few agents are undertaking production opportunities: they all view these opportunities as "too costly." Here there are certainly gains to trade if only agents could coordinate their production decisions. The presumption of this model is that the costs of this type of coordination are prohibitive. Further, there is no "Walrasian auctioneer" to coordinate trades. The results are the possibility of multiple Pareto-ranked equilibria and the consequent chance of coordination failure.

DYNAMICS AND TRADING COSTS

In a series of papers, Howitt [1985] and Howitt and McAfee [1988] study economies in which there are explicit transaction costs associated with trades in labor and goods. These costs are meant to represent the search

---

4. See eq. (20) in Diamond [1982].

and recruiting processes stemming from transactions in these various markets. In keeping with the theme of complementarity, these papers generally assume that the magnitude of these costs is influenced by the level of aggregate activity. As a consequence, there are natural thick market effects at work: the higher the level of activity, the lower the transaction costs.

Howitt [1985] studies a static economy where households and firms expend effort to engage in market transactions. By assumption, the representative firm faces lower transaction costs if the representative household exerts more effort. Further, the representative firm faces higher transaction costs if other firms exert more effort. Thus the economy exhibits both a source of complementarity, between a firm and the households, and a source of substitutability, between a firm and the other firms.

Howitt characterizes the equilibrium of the model assuming that the effort of households is simply proportional to the level of their own activity. This specification thus highlights the interaction between firms. Howitt further assumes that the complementarity through the household effort dominates the congestion effect of the interfirm interaction. As a consequence, the technology describing the transaction costs implies that at higher levels of economic activity, trading costs are lower. A similar structure is used to describe the costs of trading in the labor market. Not surprisingly, there are multiple, Pareto-ranked equilibria in Howitt's economy.

Howitt and McAfee [1988] take the analysis one giant step further by looking at the stability properties of these equilibria in a dynamic version of the model. In the dynamic model, there are again households and firms and trade occurs each period in two markets, labor and goods. Firms incur per unit transaction costs from goods market trades, which, again, are assumed to be a decreasing function of the level of activity (measured in terms of employment) in the production of goods. The firm also faces costs of adjusting its labor force which also depend on the level of employment. Here there is a source of substitutability since higher levels of employment economywide imply that the costs of recruitment for a firm will rise. The interesting aspect of the model is how these two sources of interaction come together to create the dynamics.

Given the adjustment cost function of the firm, it must solve a dynamic optimization problem, taking as given the time path of aggregate activity. This yields a first-order condition expressed in the form of a Euler equation. The equilibrium condition, that the representative firm and the average over the firms are the same, is then imposed on this dynamic equation. This is essentially the approach used in the Baxter–King model described in Chapter 3.

Howitt and McAfee are then left with a second-order differential equation describing the equilibria of the economy. This then permits a characterization of the steady states of the system as well as an evaluation of the local dynamics, a key point of this analysis. In fact, Howitt and McAfee put some structure on the production and transaction cost technologies so that there will generally be multiple steady states. But what are the stability properties of these steady states?

Interestingly, they find that the low level equilibrium, in which there is little employment so that transaction costs are high, may be locally stable. So, for any value of employment in the neighborhood of the low level steady state equilibrium, there will exist a continuum of paths leading back to this steady state. This local stability apparently derives from the dynamic interaction of firms since the gains to large expansions today depend not only on the current level of activity but also on the expectations of the future. Given the basic indeterminacy of future activity, the paths of employment creating local stability can be self-fulfilling.

MONEY AND SEARCH

In Diamond's model the emphasis is on the multiplicity of equilibria created in a search environment. In a series of papers, Kiyotaki and Wright [1989, 1993] use a related model to study the transaction role of fiat money. This model provides another setting in which complementarities are present since the usefulness of money as a medium of exchange depends on the number of other agents using money for transactions. At one extreme, money can have no value at all simply because no one believes it will serve as a medium of exchange. At the other extreme, fiat money can (almost) replace barter as a means of exchange. This monetary equilibrium is of considerable interest as this is one of the few environments which can produce, in a general equilibrium setting, a demand for fiat money. In particular, no constraints that money must be used in exchange are employed. The value of money for exchange purposes is entirely an endogenous outcome.

Our analysis of the value of money will follow Kiyotaki and Wright [1993] by first exploring the structure of barter trades in an economy without fiat money. This is a useful starting point as it illuminates the double coincidence of wants problem. In fact, the benefits from overcoming this problem generate a role for fiat money. So, after discussing the barter economy, fiat money is introduced and equilibria exist in which otherwise useless pieces of paper have value.

Barter Economy

To motivate barter trade, it is necessary to have some heterogeneity in tastes and endowments. Yet, for tractability, it is useful to stay close to the representative agent structure by assumptions of symmetry. The basic environment accomplishes these objectives. There is a continuum of commodities and agents distributed uniformly on a unit circle. All goods are indivisible and appear in units of size 1. Following Kiyotaki and Wright, let u be the utility an agent receives from consuming a good that is at most a distance x from his location on the circle. Goods that are further away than this critical distance provide no direct utility to the agent. Assume that $0 < x < 1$ so that individuals do not consume all goods but derive utility from a measurable subset of the goods. In this way, x is a measure of the dispersion or differentiation of tastes in the economy.

Individuals can be in one of two states. As in Diamond's model studied in the previous chapter, either they are traders searching for a trading partner or they are searching for a production opportunity. For simplicity, production while searching for a trading partner is precluded.

Let α represent the probability that an agent without any goods to trade locates a production opportunity in a given period. Normalize utility so that production is costless. We discuss later a model that integrates the participation decision of the Diamond model with the more complex trading environment studied by Kiyotaki and Wright. Finding a production opportunity implies that the agent will become a trader in the following period, in search of a trading partner, as consumption of the good one produces is again precluded.

An agent with a unit of the good to trade is assumed to match with a trading partner with probability ρ. Kiyotaki and Wright assume that there exists a trading cost of ε with $0 < \varepsilon < u$. In this case, trades will rise only between two agents who have a "double coincidence of wants." This occurs when two traders meet and each derives utility from the good the other is holding. Since all goods are equally likely to be produced in this economy and agents are uniformly distributed along the unit circle, two randomly matched traders will have gains to trade with probability x^2. Thus the magnitude of the double coincidence of wants problem is neatly parameterized in this economy.

Let V_p be the value of lifetime utility of being a producer in search of a trading opportunity, and let V_G be the value of lifetime utility of being a trader with goods in inventory.[5] Then, in this economy without fiat money,

$$V_p = \beta[\alpha V_G + (1 - \alpha)V_p] \tag{5}$$

and

$$V_G = \rho x^2(u - \varepsilon + \beta V_p) + [\rho(1 - x^2) + (1 - \rho)]\beta V_G \tag{6}$$

When an agent is in the production state, a production opportunity arises with probability α, in which case the agent becomes a goods trader next period; however, with probability $(1 - \alpha)$ no production opportunity appears. Once the agent has goods, a trading partner is found with probability ρ and with probability x^2 there is a double coincidence of wants and a trade occurs. The agent is then in the production state in the following period. Otherwise, the agent searches again for a trading partner.

The equilibrium values associated with the two states can be obtained by solving these two equations simultaneously. In the special case where production opportunities always appear ($\alpha = 1$), $V_G = \rho x^2(u - \varepsilon)/((1 - \beta)(1 + \beta \rho x^2))$ and $V_p = \beta V_G$. Both V_p and V_G are increasing in ρx^2.

Note that in this economy, no single good serves as commodity money. As Kiyotaki and Wright emphasize, the equilibrium characterized here treats all commodities symmetrically. In fact, as argued in Kiyotaki and Wright [1989], it is possible for one good to emerge as a commodity money in this environment, thus facilitating exchange.

Fiat Money

In this economy there may be value in fiat money as it prevents the double coincidence of wants problem that arises from $x < 1$. Money facilitates exchange to the extent that trade can arise when two agents who lack a double coincidence of wants will nonetheless be willing to trade. One

---

5. For the expressions that follow, we are using a discrete time approach and assuming that trades occur in the period when two trading partners meet. This contrasts with the continuous time formulation presentation of Diamond's model in the previous chapter and in Kiyotaki–Wright. We choose the discrete time formulation since it facilitates a more intuitive presentation of the flows between states.

agent will consume the good held by the other and will provide money in exchange for this good. These trades are rational only if the agent receiving money does so in anticipation of trading money for goods in the future. So, as in the standard overlapping generations model, money has value in this economy only to the extent that all agents believe it has value. That is, the value of money is sustained solely through the beliefs of the traders. The fragile nature of monetary equilibria is made clear by the fact that in any economy with valued fiat money, there will always exist an equilibrium in which money is worthless.

To characterize the monetary economy, assume that a fraction M of the agents are initially holders of fiat money and the remainder are given a unit endowment of the good. In order to prevent problems of bargaining and inventory holdings of multiple goods, assume that money is also indivisible so that all trades involve either the exchange of a unit of one good for another or the exchange of a unit of money for a unit of the good.[6] Thus the price of goods in terms of fiat money is set at unity. In contrast to barter exchange, there are no transaction costs associated with exchanges involving money.

In a stationary equilibrium with valued fiat money, denote by υ the fraction of traders (those in search of a trading partner) who are holding money and call these *money traders*. The remaining traders hold a unit of some commodity and are consequently called *commodity traders*. In contrast to the model without money, traders must decide what actions to take in the event they meet another trader. The choice of whether to trade or not depends on what the other trader has to offer, money or goods. Since there is a transaction cost associated with the exchange of goods for goods, the only nonmonetary exchanges that occur in a *monetary equilibrium* will involve traders who are each willing to consume the other's good. Thus the only nontrivial choice occurs when a money trader and a commodity trader meet. If the money trader values the good held by the commodity trader, will an exchange occur? Denote by π the probability that an arbitrary goods trader is willing to exchange goods for money and let Π be the aggregate proportion of goods traders willing to make that exchange.

Given Π, the value functions for an agent who accepts money for goods with probability π are

---

6. Recent work by Trejos–Wright [1995] extends these models to incorporate bargaining so that prices are not determined by these restrictions on inventory holding.

$$V_p = \beta[\alpha V_G + (1 - \alpha)V_p] \tag{7}$$

$$V_G = \rho(1 - v)[x^2(u - \varepsilon + \beta V_p) + (1 - x^2)\beta V_G] \tag{8}$$
$$+ \rho v[\beta x(\pi V_m + (1 - \pi)V_G) + (1 - x)\beta V_G] + (1 - \rho)V_G$$

$$V_M = \rho(1 - v)[x\Pi(u - \varepsilon + \beta V_p) + ((1 - x) + x(1 - \Pi))\beta V_M] \tag{9}$$
$$+ \rho v\beta V_M + (1 - \rho)V_M$$

The first expression indicates, as in the earlier model, that the value of being in the production state is that with probability α there will be a change in state to a goods trader in the next period.

The value of being a goods trader, the second expression, has three terms which represent the three possible outcomes for such an agent. First, the agent is matched with another goods trader with probability $\rho(1 - v)$. Given this, with probability x^2 there is a double coincidence of wants so that trade occurs between the two agents. In this case, both receive $(u - \varepsilon)$ from the exchange and the agent starts to search for a production opportunity in the next period. If there is not a double coincidence of wants (which happens with probability $(1 - x^2)$), the goods trader remains in that state. With probability ρv the goods trader meets a money trader. Given this, with probability x the goods trader has a product that the money trader desires and a trade occurs with probability π. Otherwise, there is not even a single coincidence of wants and no trade occurs. We will discuss the determination of π in a moment. Finally, with probability $(1 - \rho)$ the goods trader meets no one so that there is no change in the state of the agent.

The value of being a money trader is given in the third expression. With probability $\rho(1 - v)$ the money trader meets a goods trader. With probability x, the money trader desires the good held by the goods trader. With probability Π, an aggregate variable, the goods trader will accept money for goods. If an exchange occurs, the money trader enjoys the consumption (less the transactions cost) and changes to the production state. Otherwise, the money trader stays in the same state.

As noted earlier, one equilibrium in this model is for money to have no value. That is, $\Pi = \pi = 0$.[7] Clearly, if no other agents are accepting money in exchange for goods ($\Pi = 0$), then the optimal choice of an individual agent is not to exchange goods for money either ($\pi = 0$) since fiat money has no value when it is not used for exchange purposes. This

---

7. Note, though, that the economy with money in which it has no value is not quite the same as an economy without money unless those with the worthless money can discard it and find a production opportunity.

can be seen directly from the three expressions by noting that at $\Pi = 0$, $V_M = 0$ is the only solution to (9).

An intermediate equilibrium obtains when $\pi = \Pi = x$ so that both money and goods are equally likely to be exchangeable for a desired good. Hence a trader is indifferent between holding goods and holding money in searching for a trading partner. Formally, one can use (7) to (9) to see that at $\Pi = x$, π is indeterminate.

A final equilibrium occurs when money is used for exchange whenever a money trader and a goods trader meet, i.e., $\Pi = 1$. To verify that this is an equilibrium, we must show that the best response of an individual agent to $\Pi = 1$ is to set $\pi = 1$. Clearly, $\pi = 1$ if $V_m \geq V_G$. From manipulation of (7)–(9), one can see that $V_m > V_G$ when $\Pi = 1$ since $x < 1$ by assumption. Intuitively, a goods trader will exchange goods for money since the likelihood of being able to exchange money for goods is larger than the likelihood of exchanging goods for goods since the latter requires the double coincidence of wants while the former does not.

From the viewpoint of coordination models and strategic complementarities, this economy has upward sloping reaction curves. Consider the relationship between the economywide acceptability of money, Π, and the individual optimal choice, $\pi^*(\Pi)$. The preceding arguments indicate that $\pi^*(1) = 1$ and $\pi^*(0) = 0$. Kiyotaki and Wright show that $\pi^*(\Pi)$ is a nondecreasing function: it is 0 for low values of Π, 1 for high values of Π and there is indifference at the individual level for one value of Π.

In terms of coordination failures, Kiyotaki and Wright first consider the extreme case of $\alpha = 1$ so that production opportunities arise with certainty and, in their continuous time version of the model, without delay. In this case, the acceptability of money yields a Pareto improvement. In particular, commodity traders and money traders are all strictly better off in an equilibrium in which money is acceptable for all trades ($\pi = \Pi = 1$) than in the nonmonetary equilibrium.

Further, even in $\alpha < 1$, Kiyotaki and Wright are able to make statements about ex ante expected utility, i.e., the welfare of an individual prior to the allocation of initial endowments of goods and money, as the stock of money varies. For equilibria with $\pi = \Pi = 0$ and $\pi = \Pi = x$, increases in the stock of money are not desirable since this crowds out commodity traders (it is not feasible to hold money and goods) without providing a lubricant for trade. In the $\pi = \Pi = 1$ equilibrium, the optimal proportion of money traders in the economy depends on the extent of differentiation in tastes. If $x \geq \frac{1}{2}$, then it is optimal not to introduce money into the economy. Otherwise, pure barter is not very efficient because of the low probability of there being a double coincidence of wants so that the existence of some amount of money is desirable.

Money and Production

It is interesting to consider how the introduction of money impacts on production decisions. Kiyotaki and Wright investigate the relationship between specialization of labor and money. The idea here is that money can provide an incentive for agents to become more specialized in the type of good they produce. That is, as noted earlier, money is much more valuable in facilitating exchange if x, a measure of the specificity of commodities, is low. In the other direction, the returns to specialization may be larger in a monetary economy since the double coincidence of wants problem is not as strong. To model this, Kiyotaki and Wright assume that the likelihood of finding a production opportunity (a proxy of the cost) decreases with x. Hence goods that are more specialized, in that they appeal to fewer agents, are less expensive to produce: specialized production is less costly. They find that money facilitates the specialization of production in that the degree of specialization is greatest in a monetary economy.

Johri [1997] pursues the connection between money and aggregate economy activity by considering a merger of the Diamond economy studied earlier with that studied by Kiyotaki and Wright. In particular, suppose that production opportunities arrive with probability α but that there is a cost c associated with production. Further, as in Diamond [1982], assume that these costs are distributed according to a cumulative distribution function, $F(c)$. Otherwise, the model is as stated in Kiyotaki and Wright so that the chance of meeting a trading partner, ρ, is independent of the number of other agents searching for a trading partner.

For this economy, the value of searching for a production opportunity is given by

$$V_p = \alpha \int_0^{c^*} (-c + \beta V_G)\, dF(c) + [\alpha(1 - F(c^*)) + (1 - \alpha)]V_p \qquad (10)$$

Otherwise, the expressions for the values of being money and goods traders given earlier do not change. The issue here is whether the existence of money enhances production.

To investigate this, we know from the earlier analysis of the Diamond model that there will exist a critical production cost, c^*_b, such that in the economy without money, only production opportunities at or below this cost will be undertaken. Similarly, for this economy there exists a cutoff cost in which money is universally acceptable, c^*_m. Johri shows that the presence of money excites economic activity. This is a consequence of the fact that $c^*_m > c^*_b$ for small quantities of money: more expensive production opportunities are undertaken in the monetary economy.

SUMMARY

This chapter provided a series of models that emphasize complementarities through the costs of trading. In some models, such as those pursued by Howitt and Howitt and McAfee, there are specific trading cost functions that include a "thick markets" effect: trading costs are lower the higher is the volume of trade. The Diamond model puts more structure on the problem by assuming a search environment in which trading probabilities depend on the fraction of traders in different states. Building on this environment, Kiyotaki and Wright have produced a search theoretic model of money demand.

Relative to the production complementarities model, the search model is unexplored territory. This is partly because there are no dynamic stochastic versions of, say, the Diamond model which are analogous to the Baxter–King extension of the basic stochastic growth model. Further, the estimation of these thick market effects is not quite as easy as putting an extra argument into a production function.

Yet, these models offer great promise since they rest upon a fundamental trading friction: the spatial distribution of agents. With this friction comes the need for a mechanism to bring agents together, and it is apparent that coordination problems may emerge along the way.

6   Timing of Discrete Choices

One feature of aggregate behavior is the synchronization of discrete decisions such as the purchase of durable capital by firms and durable goods by households.[1] These expenditures are important to understand in that they are extremely volatile elements of aggregate spending. Put differently, these are the elements of total expenditure that display the most time series variance. Introducing these discrete choices into traditional general equilibrium models is somewhat difficult because of the nonconvexity associated with lumpy expenditures on consumer and firm durables. One means of dealing with these nonconvexities is to look for equilibria in which there is some "smoothing by aggregation." The effect of doing so, however, is that these discrete choices are, by construction, no longer synchronized so that their macroeconomic importance is dramatically reduced. In fact, this approach works only if agents have an incentive to take actions at different points in time.

When, in contrast, agents have an incentive to synchronize their discrete choices, then smoothing by aggregation is no longer possible. In this case, synchronized discrete decisions can matter for the macroeconomy. They can create endogenous fluctuations of the aggregate economy and magnify underlying disturbances to that economy.

The focus of this chapter is on the basis for synchronization and, more generally, the issue of the timing of economic activity. The first part of

---

1. Cooper, Haltiwanger and Power [1997] document the fact that large bursts of investment at the plant level are a major fraction of overall manufacturing investment. See, for example, Lam [1991] for evidence on durables.

the chapter looks at incentives for the synchronization of activity. The second part goes on to explore the issue of delay.

SIMPLE GAMES OF TIMING

We first describe two simple games of timing, presented in Cooper and Haltiwanger [1992] and Cahuc and Kempf [1997], to understand better the incentive to synchronize decisions. These two models reach rather different conclusions and it is constructive to understand the distinct forces at work.

Fluctuating Endowments

Consider an infinitely repeated noncooperative game played by two agents, indexed by $i = 1, 2$. Player 1's payoffs for period t are given by $\pi^1 (y(t), z(t))$ where $y(t)$ is agent 1's period t endowment and $z(t)$ is the endowment of player 2 in period t. Player 2's preferences are defined analogously. The interaction between the endowments in the players' payoffs is intended to succinctly represent consumption complementarities, a trading complementarity or some form of demand spillover, as in the various models presented in earlier chapters. At this stage, our focus is on the implications rather than the source of the interaction.

Suppose that the endowment process fluctuates deterministically so that each agent has a high quantity, H, in one period followed by a low quantity, L, in the next, and then the process repeats. Agents are assumed to discount the future at rate β. Further, we assume that goods are not storable.

The agents play a game of timing in which they choose whether to have their period of high endowment in even or odd periods. That is, the strategy space for each agent is $\{E, 0\}$. For example, if both players select E, then both receive their high endowments in even periods. This is a simple device for modeling decisions to stagger or synchronize. These choices are made simultaneously and prior to the first period. To maintain symmetry between these choices, after the choices are made, nature flips a fair coin to determine whether the first period will be even or odd. If the Nash equilibrium entails both players' having high endowment in even or odd periods, then we term this a *synchronized* equilibrium. If one player chooses high endowment in even (odd) periods and his opponent chooses to receive the high endowment in odd (even) periods, then a *staggered* equilibrium results.

Formally,

Proposition 1 (Cooper–Haltiwanger [1992]): *If* $\pi_{12} > 0$ $(\pi_{12} < 0)$, *then the players will synchronize (stagger) high production.*

Proof: Suppose that both players synchronize their production; then the lifetime expected (because of nature's coin flip) discounted utility is

$$V^{sy} = \{\pi(H, H) + \pi(L, L)\}/2(1 - \beta).$$

Alternatively, if the players stagger, then the lifetime expected discounted utility for each is given by

$$V^{st} = \{\pi(H, L) + \pi(L, H)\}/2(1 - \beta).$$

The difference between the payoffs from synchronization and staggering, $V^{sy} - V^{st} \equiv \Delta$, is given by

$$\int_{L}^{H}\int_{L}^{H} \pi_{12}(x, z)dx\, dz$$

Hence if $\pi_{12} > 0$ $(\pi_{12} < 0)$, $\Delta > (<) 0$ and the players will synchronize (stagger) periods of high production.   QED.

The intuition behind this result is straightforward. Strategic complementarities ($\pi_{12} > 0$) imply that each agent prefers to have a large value of the endowment when the other does as well: i.e., the marginal payoff from high endowment increases with the quantity given to the other agent. In contrast, strategic substitutability implies that the marginal gain from high endowment is lower when the other agent has high endowment as well. Thus, the equilibrium is to stagger in this case.

From the perspective of macroeconomics, this example is relatively uninteresting since it attributes all fluctuations to random variations in endowments. However, as discussed later, it is possible to use this result to provide some insights into discrete decisions on investment, production runs, the introduction of new inventions, and so forth, which are important aggregate variables. In all cases, the desire to synchronize is driven by the presence of strategic complements in the reduced form payoffs of the players.

Dynamic Strategic Interactions

The example of the timing of random endowments highlights the gains to synchronization in the presence of complementarity. However, the game is quite simple in that the endowment process is itself exogenous, implying that agents' choices influence the timing but not the magnitude of their consumption. Thus, the interaction concerns only the timing of the "high action." A richer structure is investigated by Cahuc and Kempf [1997] along the lines of Maskin and Tirole [1987, 1988a, 1988b].

Consider an infinite horizon game played by two agents, $i = 1, 2$. Time is discrete and indexed by $t = 0, 1, 2, \ldots$. Each player selects an action, a_i, from the interval $[0, 1]$. Preferences for player $i = 1, 2$ within period t are given by $v_{it} = v(a^t_i, a^t_{-i})$ where $v(\cdot)$ is strictly increasing and strictly concave in its first argument. Here $-i$ denotes the choice of the other player. Lifetime utility for player $i = 1, 2$ is given by $\sum \delta^t v_{it}$ where $\delta \, \varepsilon \, (0, 1)$. Note that the payoffs for the two agents are assumed to be the same.

Cahuc and Kempf consider the steady states of two alternative timing structures. For both, agents choose an action that is in effect for two periods. One can think of this as reflecting some form of adjustment cost, though these costs generally imply state dependent rather than time dependent policies.

Under a regime of *synchronization*, agents choose simultaneously; under a regime of *staggering*, one agent chooses ahead of the other. Note that the timing here has an implication not explored in the Cooper–Haltiwanger structure: as there are only two agents, the agent choosing must *internalize* the response of the other when actions are staggered.

Synchronized equilibria are relatively easy to characterize since agents move simultaneously and their actions are in effect, by assumption, for two periods. Let $\phi(a_{-i})$ represent the best response of player i to the other's action. Assume that $\phi(0) > 0$, $\phi(1) < 1$ and that the slope of the reaction function is everywhere less than 1 in absolute value. These conditions are sufficient to guarantee the existence of a unique symmetric Nash equilibrium given by an action a^* such that $v_1(a^*, a^*) = 0$ or, equivalently, $\phi(a^*) = a^*$. So in the steady state of the synchronized equilibrium, both players choose a^* each period.

Staggered equilibria, in contrast, require agents to be forward looking in their behavior. A player choosing an action this period must recognize that the other player, who will choose an action in the next period, will optimally respond to whatever action is taken today. Thus each player must take into account the reaction function of the other. So, the reaction function, which we denote by $R(a)$, is the central element in the analysis. Since the agents are identical and time has no direct effect on preferences analysis, we search for a stationary symmetric equilibrium. Further, since the choices are staggered we have imposed the restriction that the choice of a player depends only on the current action (chosen in the previous period) by the other player.

More formally, it is natural to look for equilibria that are termed *Markov perfect equilibria*. The equilibria are Markov in the sense that the action of the player that moves in the current period depends on the state of the game, given by the action of the player moving in the previous period. The criterion of perfection is met by requiring the agent to predict the other player's response to an action chosen in the current period correctly.

Following the presentation in Cahuc and Kempf, a symmetric Markov perfect equilibrium is thus characterized by a reaction function $R(a)$ and two value functions, $W(a)$ and $V(a)$, such that

$$R(a_j) = \mathrm{argmax}_{a_i} v(a_i, a_j) + \delta W(a_i) \tag{1}$$

where player i is selecting an action (a_i) given the choice of player j (a_j) from the previous period. Let $V(a_j)$ be the utility level from the solution of the optimization problem in (1).

In this problem, $W(a_i)$ represents the value to the player of the game given his choice of action, a_i. That is, this is the value to player i of continuing the game when the other player chooses, given the choice of a_i in the previous period. So,

$$W(a_i) = v(a_i, R(a_i)) + \delta\ V(R(a_i)) \tag{2}$$

where the function $R(a_i)$ represents the response of player j to the action of i. Note that in the symmetric equilibria, this reaction function is the same as that characterized in (1).

So, to make clear the nature of the interactions again, consider the choice of player i in a period where it is player i's turn to move. Player j selected an action last period; call it a_j. Given this action, player i chooses a_i to maximize the sum of utility from this period and from the continuation of the game next period, when player j moves. This is the point of (1), where the function $W(\cdot)$ represents the value of the game starting next period in state a_i. This value, in turn, depends on the response of player j to the action taken by i, i.e., the $R(a_i)$ in (2). Finally, the value of the continuation depends on the utility flow to agent i when that agent moves again. But this is simply the value of the optimization problem in (1) with the state described by the best response of j to the action taken by i, $R(a_i)$.

Cahuc and Kempf assume that preferences are quadratic and prove that the steady state symmetric equilibrium for this game is the action level $\hat{a}$ that satisfies

$$(1 + \delta)v_1(\hat{a}, \hat{a}) + (1 + \delta)\beta \, \delta \, v_2(\hat{a}, \hat{a}) = 0 \tag{3}$$

Here β is the slope of the reaction curve at the equilibrium point which is assumed to lie between -1 and 1.

To understand this condition, consider the effects on lifetime utility of slightly changing the current action of a player. Since this change is in effect for two periods, the direct utility effect is given by the first term of (3). This change in the action will also lead the other player to alter his action in the next period. The magnitude of this reaction is given by β. From the one-period delay it is multiplied by δ and multiplied again by $(1 + \delta)$ since the response of the other agent lasts for two periods. Finally, the v_2 term captures the effect on utility of the other player's response to the deviation. The effect of this deviation is limited to these three periods since the agent that initiated the deviation reoptimizes after two periods.

One interesting question concerns the relative levels of activity in the two scenarios. As we shall see, the answer depends on the nature of both the spillovers and the strategic interaction of the two players. Relatedly, it will be useful to know which type of equilibrium yields higher payoffs to the players.

To obtain and understand these results, we use the cooperative outcome of the simultaneous move game as a benchmark. The cooperative effort level A satisfies the condition

$$v_1(A, A) + v_2(A, A) = 0 \tag{4}$$

This is directly comparable to the conditions for synchronized and staggered equilibria as used in the construction of Table 6.1.[2]

---

2. These comparisons use the assumption that the reaction curve has a slope less than 1 in absolute value at the unique equilibrium point in the synchronized game.

Table 6.1

	strategic complements	strategic substitutes
positive spillovers	$A > â > a^*$	$A > a^* > â$
negative spillovers	$a^* > â > A$	$â > a^* > A$

The results of Cahuc and Kempf can be summarized in Table 6.1. To understand this table, recall that a^* is the synchronized equilibrium while $â$ is the equilibrium with staggering.

Consider first the case of strategic complements and positive spillovers. In the synchronized equilibrium, each player would prefer (given the positive spillovers) that the other take a higher action but neither has the capacity to motivate the other to do so since they move simultaneously. In the staggered equilibrium, they have an opportunity to provide this incentive. By increasing their effort levels above the synchronized equilibrium, each player elicits increased effort by the other to take advantage of the positive spillover effects. Of course each agent has an incentive to reciprocate because of the strategic complementarity. Thus a higher action is observed in the staggered equilibrium than in the synchronized equilibrium in the case of positive spillovers and strategic complements.

If spillovers were positive but interactions were strategic substitutes, then each player would wish the other to put forth more effort. In the staggering game, the players create this response by working less.

The welfare results under the two alternative timing structures basically mirror the ordering of activity levels given in Table 6.1. Cahuc and Kempf (see their Proposition 2) argue that welfare is higher under synchronization iff the game exhibits strategic substitutability. From the table, we see that the equilibrium under synchronization (a^*) is closer to the cooperative effort level iff the game is one of strategic substitutability. For example, if there are positive spillovers and strategic substitutes, then action levels with synchronization are too low relative to the cooperative solution. If agents stagger, they will each try to motivate the other to take higher action by lowering his action. Thus, $a^* > â$ and welfare is lower under staggering. Evidently, the opportunity to influence the action of the other implies that, in equilibrium, both players are worse off! Alternatively, if there is strategic complementarity, then staggering brings the equilibrium of the game closer to the cooperative outcome so that welfare is higher.

Given this welfare ordering, Cahuc and Kempf allow players the opportunity to choose whether to move in, say, even or odd periods, as in the discussion of the previous section. Not surprisingly, players will choose to synchronize iff their interaction is characterized by strategic substitutes.

Interestingly, this analysis suggests almost exactly the opposite conclusion from that of Cooper and Haltiwanger. The difference, of course, lies in the nature of the strategic interaction across players and the choice sets of the agents.

IMPLEMENTATION DECISIONS

Given the role of strategic complementarity in the synchronization result, it is useful to recall that we have already seen numerous examples of economies in which strategic complementarity naturally emerges. In one case of interest the spending patterns of agents across sectors create these complementarities, as in the models explored in Chapter 4.

We now turn to a fascinating model by Shleifer [1986] which uses these demand linkages to create incentives for the bunching (synchronization) of innovations. The model has the important feature that discrete activities (the introduction of innovations) are synchronized even though the inventions that underlie these innovations are staggered, so that, from the perspective of the aggregate economy, the exogenous process of invention is completely smooth. Still, some of the equilibria of the model exhibit endogenous cycles as a result of the synchronization of discrete activities. In this way, cycles are not the consequence of the assumption of cyclical inventions but rather emerge endogenously.

Shleifer [1986] considers a model in which there are S sectors of economic activity. Within each sector, there are a large number of firms who produce an identical product and compete using price as a strategy variable. As agents are very small in this economy, the strategic interactions highlighted by Cahuc and Kempf do not appear in this analysis.

In each period, a single firm in a fraction of the sectors receives a new invention. In particular, let n denote the number of sectors receiving an invention in a given period. Thus, the time between inventions to a sector will be S/n.

Three points are important here. First, only one firm in each of the sectors receives the invention so that this single firm has the ability, assuming no capacity constraints, to take over the market and use its technological advantage to exert monopoly power. Second, the fact that only a fraction of the sectors receives new inventions in each period implies that the underlying process of technological advance is partially staggered by assumption. As a consequence, the bunching of innovations will reflect the choice to synchronize rather than the presence of economy-wide technological change. As we shall see, the interactions of the agents in the economy can produce a solution in which innovations are more synchronized than inventions as a result of the presence of complementarities across sectors. Third, the order of the inventions is strictly exogenous: the agents in the economy cannot time inventions to coincide with slumps or booms in aggregate activity.

An invention in each sector increases the productivity of labor by $\mu > 1$ so that the firm receiving the invention can produce output with $1/\mu$ of the labor that competitors in the same sector use. Once an innovation is introduced to the market, the firm will price output slightly below the common marginal cost of its rivals. In this way, the firm captures the entire market. This is the profit maximizing price since, as we shall see, the aggregate demand for any industry is unitary elastic so that a monopolist would have an incentive to charge an infinite price. Shleifer [1986] assumes that immediately after innovation, the firm's rivals in the industry imitate the invention so that monopoly profits exist for only a single period.

The key insight into the model is that firms have an incentive to time the introduction of the new technique when aggregate demand is high so that profit, which we shall see is proportional to aggregate demand, is high as well. Further, as demonstrated below, aggregate demand depends on the total level of profit in the economy. Subject to some conditions on the behavior of interest rates, firms choose to synchronize innovations and this gives rise to Shleifer's implementation cycles.

Consumption and Savings Decisions

The complementarity in the model, and thus the basis for the synchronization, is derived from the behavior of the representative consumer and the implementation decision of the firm. In period t, the representative consumer earns income (y_t) from labor inelastically supplied to the market (L) and receives all of the profits in the economy, Π_t. Preferences of the agents are given by

$$\sum_{t=1}^{\infty} \rho^{t-1} \frac{c_t^{1-\gamma}}{1-\gamma} \tag{5}$$

where c_t is an index of period t consumption given by

$$c_t = \prod_{j=1}^{s} c_{tj}^{\lambda} \tag{6}$$

and c_{tj} is the period t consumption of good j and $\lambda = 1/S$. Thus intratemporal preferences are Cobb–Douglas while intertemporal preferences have the familiar constant relative risk aversion (CRRA) formulation. The budget constraint for intertemporal optimization is given by

$$\sum_{t=1}^{\infty} \left(\frac{y_t - \sum_{j=1}^{s} p_{tj} c_{tj}}{R_t} \right) = 0 \tag{7}$$

where R_t is the interest rate on a t-period loan.

The demand functions for these preferences take the usual constant budget shares form: $p_{tj} c_{tj} = \lambda y_t$. Shleifer assumes that there is no capital or any other store of value so that, in equilibrium, interest rates adjust to ensure that desired savings is zero. In particular, the period t interest rate satisfies

$$1 + r_t = \frac{1}{\rho} \left(\frac{y_{t+1}}{y_t} \right)^{\gamma} \frac{\left(\prod_{j=1}^{s} p_{t+1j}^{\lambda} \right)^{1-\gamma}}{\left(\prod_{j=1}^{s} p_{tj}^{\lambda} \right)^{1-\gamma}} \tag{8}$$

From this expression, variations in both total income and prices will influence the real interest rate. Holding prices fixed, an increase in period $t + 1$ income will induce a rise in the interest rate since consumers will increase period t consumption in response to a rise in anticipated future income. Since there is no store of value in the economy, interest rates must rise to induce savings. The rise of the interest rate is determined by the curvature of the utility function, parameterized by ρ.

As we shall see, the interaction of the firms within a sector will determine the price of each good in every period. Given those prices and the resulting income, this equation will determine the interest rate. Of course, part of the determination of output and prices involves a firm's choice on the timing of implementing an invention, which, as discussed later, depends on the pattern of interest rates.

Implementation Decisions

The key to the model is the choice of the timing of implementation by a firm receiving an invention. Suppose that aggregate demand is Y and that other firms in the sector produce at a cost (in labor terms) of w. Thus, the cost per unit of output for the innovating firm is w/μ. The innovating firm will receive all of the spending on this sector by pricing goods at w. Therefore, the profit for the innovating firm will be

$$\lambda Y - \left(\lambda \frac{Y}{w}\right)\left(\frac{w}{\mu}\right) = \frac{\lambda(\mu - 1)Y}{\mu} = mY \qquad (9)$$

where λ was defined earlier as $1/S$, i.e., the fraction of total income spent on each sector and $m = \lambda(\mu - 1)/\mu$.

The important aspect of this expression is that the profit of the innovating firm is proportional to the level of aggregate demand Y. Thus, factors that increase aggregate demand in any particular period make the introduction of inventions in that period more profitable. Since aggregate demand depends on total profits, periods of high profits are also times of high demand. Finally, since profits are high when firms are introducing innovations, there is a gain to introducing new inventions when others are doing so as this is a time of overall high aggregate demand. This is the incentive for the synchronization of innovations. Of course, as a result of discounting, there are some costs to not introducing inventions immediately, and it is this tradeoff we turn to next.

Equilibria

An equilibrium is a sequence of prices, interest rates, consumption and implementation decisions such that all markets clear in every period. There is one equilibrium in the model which does not display any synchronization at all. In this equilibrium, all firms introduce inventions at the time they are received. Along this equilibrium path, there are no booms in aggregate demand so that the incentives for delaying innovations to synchronize with others do not arise. That is, consider the decision of a firm in any sector which has just received an invention. Since all other firms are implementing inventions immediately, the level of aggregate demand is constant. So, this particular firm perceives no gain to delay since, being small, it takes the level of aggregate demand in each period as given. Thus, as long as the interest rate is positive, the firm will also choose to implement inventions immediately.[3]

Other equilibria which display synchronization can exist. Consider cycles of period T in which inventions are accumulated for at most T periods and then are implemented simultaneously. Since another invention will be introduced in a given sector after S/n periods, Shleifer looks for cycles such that $T \leq S/n$. In the period after a boom (the period after implementation), there is massive imitation by producers in each sector and a new cycle begins. For a T cycle to exist, it must be the case that firms receiving inventions prior to a boom must have an incentive to delay the introduction of new inventions and also have an incentive to introduce these inventions when others are doing so rather than delaying further.

In the candidate T cycle, denote aggregate profits in the boom period by Π_T. From (9), the profit of an innovating firm is $\pi_t = my_T$ where $m = \lambda(\mu - 1)/\mu$ and y_T is the level of aggregate demand in the boom. Since there are n firms receiving inventions each period and T periods between the booms, aggregate profits are given by $\Pi_T = nT\pi_t = nTmy_T$. Using the budget constraint, $y_T = L + \Pi_T$, the level of aggregate spending in a boom equals $L/(1 - nTm)$ and $\pi_T = mL/(1 - nmT)$ is the level of profit for each innovating firm in the boom period of a candidate T cycle.

Given this level of profit, does a firm want to synchronize the introduction of its invention with others? Consider the choice of a firm that receives an invention at the start of a T cycle. Should that firm delay innovation? If it does, then others receiving inventions later in the cycle will choose to delay as well since interest rates are positive.

Suppose that instead of delaying, the firm implements immediately. In this case, profits will be mL since aggregate demand is L as all other firms are delaying innovations. Delaying for anything less than T periods (when the next boom occurs) is not desirable since the delay is costly as a result of discounting. If, however, the firm delays for T periods, then the fact that demand is high in a boom may outweigh the costs of waiting that are due to discounting. The present value of the profits received in the boom (T periods hence) in π_T/R_{T-1} where is R_{T-1} discounts the flow from the

---

3. Condition (14) in Shleifer's paper guarantees that the interest rate is positive in the steady state where there is no delay in the introduction of new innovations.

boom period back to the present along the equilibrium path. A necessary condition for a T cycle is thus $\pi_T/R_{T-1} > mL$.

Using the market clearing condition and the individual's first-order condition, Shleifer shows that this condition reduces to

$$f(T) \equiv \rho^{T-1}(1 - nTm)^{\gamma-1} > 1 \qquad (10)$$

To understand this condition, note that there are two influences on the incentives to delay the introduction of inventions. The first, which promotes delay, is the fact that profits are much higher in a boom. The ratio of π_T to the profits from no delay, mL, is $1/(1 - nTm)$, which exceeds 1. The second influence is the pattern of the short-term interest rates over the T cycle, R_{T-1}.[4] In the $T-2$ periods prior to the boom, interest rates are constant as there are no fluctuations in either prices or output. In the period before the boom, however, the consumer will anticipate higher output and consumption during the boom and will, without any adjustment in the interest rate, wish to borrow against this higher future income to smooth consumption. Since borrowing and lending are impossible, interest rates must rise to offset this desire. This increase in the interest rate reduces the profitability from delay. In order to have a T boom, this increase in the interest rate must not be very big. In other words, savings must be fairly sensitive to the interest rate. As the responsiveness of savings to changes in the interest rate is partly determined by γ, the conditions for a T cycle provide a restriction that γ not be too large. So for there to be a T boom, ρ should be near 1, γ not too large and μ large so $(1 - nTm)$ will be small.

In addition to guaranteeing that no firms receiving an invention would wish to innovate immediately, it is also necessary to check that no firm wishes to wait until after the boom to introduce an invention. While demand is high during a boom, there is a gain to waiting since, in the period following a boom, there will be an economywide price reduction due to the imitation of inventions by competitors.

Shleifer shows that a sufficient condition to prevent delay beyond T periods is

$$\rho\mu^{n\lambda(1-\gamma)} < 1 \qquad (11)$$

This is a sufficient condition in that even if there is no possibility that a future firm will innovate in its sector, a given firm will choose to implement

---

4. Recall that R_t is the product of the one period interest rates from period 1 to period t, where the one period rates were given earlier from the Euler equation at the point of zero saving.

an invention in a T-period boom rather than wait for a future boom. As noted by Shleifer, this condition is equivalent to the transversality condition for the consumer's choice problem.

The main result on cycles is Shleifer's proposition indicating that given $T < S/n$, if (10) and (11) are satisfied, then there will exist a T cycle. As noted earlier, a cycle with immediate introduction of inventions ($T = 1$) will always exist. Shleifer illustrates the set of cyclical equilibria through a characterization of $f(T)$. In particular both high and low frequency cycles are possible. An interesting feature of the model is that as the length of time between cycles increases, the booms that do occur are much more intense since more inventions have been stored in anticipation of the burst in aggregate behavior.

To summarize our findings thus far, we see that in addition to the existence of equilibria with immediate innovation, there may also exist equilibria in which inventions are saved so that innovations are bunched. The gains to bunching arise from demand complementarities: since other firms are synchronizing their innovations, profits and hence aggregate demand are high. These equilibria with bunched innovations are more interesting given that the cycles are created relative to an exogenous process of staggered inventions. In this sense, the underlying interactions between agents in the model produce endogenous cycles.

From a positive perspective, the model produces an interesting link between cycles and growth. To the extent that underlying economic growth is fueled by technological progress (rather than growth of the factors of production), the model was one of the first to point out that cycles and growth are not independent processes. This theoretical point was in accord with empirical evidence that variations in output display a unit root. Hence upturns in GNP were quite persistent in the data as they are in Shleifer's model.

Given the multiplicity of equilibria, it is natural to ask about selection and welfare properties. Shleifer argues that the equilibrium with immediate introduction of inventions is the natural outcome of this economy because the resulting allocation is best for both firms and consumers. Firms prefer immediate implementation since discounted expected profits are highest. As for consumers, Shleifer shows that as long as the rate of technological progress is not too fast, consumers too will prefer the gains from immediate introduction of new products to the equilibria with cycles. While the equilibrium without cycles Pareto-dominates those with cycles, it is less obvious that this will be the natural outcome of this economy. From the experimental evidence provided earlier we know that Pareto-dominant equilibria are not always selected.

Further, Shleifer shows that if there are fixed costs to introducing innovations, firm's profits may actually be higher in a cycle. When fixed costs are present, the magnitude of the burst of activity associated with a boom is lower so that interest rates need not rise as much prior to a boom. Thus discounted profits from delay are actually larger. This further reduces the relevance of the argument that the acyclic outcome is natural in this environment.

AN EXAMPLE OF AN INDUSTRY COMPLEMENTARITY IN ACTION

The paper by Shleifer has led to related developments concerning the timing of discrete choices relative to the business cycle, two of which are described here. Cooper and Haltiwanger [1993b] investigate the timing of the replacement of existing capital with a new machine. The gain from this replacement is that a more productive machine is in use in the plant. There is a cost of replacement associated with the reduced productivity of the plant during the replacement process.

Formally, Cooper and Haltiwanger consider the following maximization problem for a single agent:

$$\max_{\{n_t\}, \{z_t\}} \sum_{t=0}^{\infty} \beta^t [u(c_t) - g(n_t)]$$

$$\text{s.t.} \qquad (12)$$

$$c_t = z_t n_t \theta_t, \qquad z_t \in \{k, 1\}, \qquad \theta_1 = \theta^* \quad \text{and}$$

$$\theta_t = \begin{cases} \rho\theta_{t-1} & \text{if } z_{t-1} = 1 \\ \theta^* & \text{if } z_{t-1} = k \end{cases}$$

In this problem, $u(c_t)$ is the utility in period t from consumption (c_t), $g(n_t)$ is the disutility of work and β is the discount rate. The production process for consumption is given in the first constraint. As there are no inventories held, output and thus consumption are equal to the product of the labor input, the productivity of the current machine (θ_t) and z_t, a choice variable that indicates whether machine replacement is occurring in period t. When $z_t = k$, machine replacement occurs in period t and labor is less productive during this period. In the following period a new machine with productivity

θ^* is in operation. When $z_t = 1$, no replacement occurs in period t and productivity falls by $\rho \in (0, 1)$ in the following period. Note that there is no technological progress in this economy, just the replacement of depreciated machinery.

The optimization problem of a single agent leads to endogenous cycles with "procyclical" output, employment and productivity. Moreover, in a stochastic version of the model, with iid shocks to tastes and the production relation, replacement is more likely to occur during periods of low labor productivity and/or low marginal utility of consumption. In this sense a theme that downturns are a good time to replace existing machinery with new, more productive equipment emerges.

Cooper and Haltiwanger then embed this problem in a multisector economy and argue that the endogenous cycle associated with machine replacement will cause similar fluctuations in other sectors of the economy. Further, if there are multiple producers simultaneously solving this machine replacement problem, then in the presence of either strategic complementarities or common shocks, individuals will have an incentive to synchronize their choices, producing interesting macroeconomic effects.

Cooper and Haltiwanger produce some empirical support for the model by investigating the seasonal pattern of production, particularly the annual shutdowns, in the automobile industry. These shutdowns are a time in which existing machinery is replaced to produce new models and to incorporate new technological advances. Cooper and Haltiwanger document the synchronization of these shutdowns across producers and find that machine replacement is more likely (and more severe) during economic downturns, as predicted by the theory.

Finally, Cooper and Haltiwanger [1993b] use a version of this model to understand the dramatic changes in the automobile industry that took place during the 1930s. Prior to 1935, the seasonal pattern of production and sales in the automobile industry included a shutdown period late in the calendar year, an automobile show in January and then a burst of sales and production in the spring. Automobile producers argued that this pattern caused excessive (and expensive) seasonal fluctuations. However, acting independently, they were apparently unable to break the seasonal pattern. Cooper and Haltiwanger argue that this reflects a complementarity through the automobile show that generated the observed synchronization. In 1935, the pattern changed as a consequence of an automobile code generated under the National Industrial Recovery Act (NIRA), which called on the producers to alter their seasonal pattern of production. The interesting aspect of this code is that the dramatic changes in the automobile industry occurred despite the fact that the NIRA had been ruled unconstitutional 6 months earlier.

DELAY

One interesting aspect of timing is the prospect of delay. Fluctuations in the levels of durable expenditures by consumers and firms may reflect their decision to delay an action until the future. This seems particularly relevant for the behavior of a firm contemplating an investment. The literature on delay is, of course, closely linked to our previous discussion on the timing of decisions.

Two types of interactions that can lead to delay have been studied in this literature. The first concerns information flows. Agents may wish to delay their actions in order to learn from others who precede them. As we shall see, this type of interaction adds to our list of sources of complementarity.[5] The second interaction we look at derives from direct production function interactions. Here delay arises because allowing others to move first will make the agent who waits more productive in the future. We look at these avenues for delay in turn.

Information Flows as a Source of Delay

This section draws upon an example in Gale [1996b] and the analysis in Chamley and Gale [1994]. To begin consider the interaction between two agents, $i = 1, 2$. Each has a discrete decision: to invest ($a_i = 1$) or not ($a_i = 0$). If agent i invests, then his payoff is $\theta_1 + \theta_2$. Assume that θ_i is uniformly distributed in the interval $[-1, 1]$ and that θ_1 and θ_2 are independent. Any player not investing receives a payoff of zero. Note that the payoffs from investment do not depend *directly* on the action of the other agent.

Each agent $i = 1, 2$ observes his own signal θ_i. Payoffs for each agent are given by the sum $\theta_1 + \theta_2$. So, each player receives a payoff relevant signal but would value knowing the signal of the other player before choosing whether or not to invest. If that signal is not directly observed, as in the model under study, then the action of the other agent will convey

5. In fact, Vives mentions this source of complementarity as well. As Gale [1996b] emphasizes, these models are closely linked to those of herd behavior and cascades explored recently by Banerjee [1992] and Bikhchandani et al. [1992].

valuable information. This specification of payoffs and the structure of information jointly create the basis of interaction between agents.

Suppose player 1 moves first after receiving the signal θ_1. Then, after observing both θ_2 and the choice of player 1, player 2 decides whether to invest or not. For now, we leave aside the question of the source of this specific timing and simply study the outcome of this game.

Given that θ_1 is uniformly distributed between $[-1, 1]$, player 1 will move iff the realized value of θ_1 exceeds 0. Surely player 1 recognizes that this decision will have an influence on the action of player 2, but that isn't important for player 1 since his payoff from action is $\theta_1 + E\theta_2 = \theta_1$ (as the θ_i's have zero unconditional mean and are uncorrelated). Since player 1 acts iff $\theta_1 > 0$, the ex ante expected utility for player 1 is $\frac{1}{4}$.[6]

The decision problem for player 2 is a bit more complicated. If player 2 observed the signal of player 1, then player 2 would invest iff $\theta_1 + \theta_2 > 0$. In this case, there would be no direct dependence of player 2 on the choice of player 1. However, in Gale's example, player 2 only observes the action of player 1 and thus must infer the value of θ_1 from this observation. Given the coarseness of the action space relative to the possible values of θ_1, player 2 will be unable to infer θ_1 from the action of player 1. Still, knowing whether or not player 1 invested is valuable to player 2.

Suppose player 2 observes that player 1 invests. Then player 2 infers $\theta_1 > 0$, so that player, upon observing θ_2, will invest iff $\theta_2 + E[\theta_1 \mid a_1 = 1] > 0$. Since $E[\theta_1 \mid a_1 = 1] = \frac{1}{2}$, player 2 will invest iff $\theta_2 > -\frac{1}{2}$. So, conditional on player 1's investing, player 2 will have an expected payoff of $\frac{9}{16}$.[7]

In contrast, if player 1 does not invest, then player 2 will require that $\theta_2 > \frac{1}{2}$ before choosing $a_2 = 1$. In this case, player's 2 expected payoff is $\frac{1}{16}$.[8]

Thus we see that player 2 is better off when player 1 invests. Further, player 2 is more likely to invest when player 1 invests. In this sense the game exhibits both positive spillovers and strategic complementarity.

One concern of course with this analysis is that the order of moves is

6. That is, the player's expected payoff conditional on investing is $\frac{1}{2}$, and the player invests with probability $\frac{1}{2}$.

7. If both players invest, then the expected payoff for player 2 is $\frac{1}{2} + E[\theta_2 > -\frac{1}{2}] = \frac{3}{4}$. Player 2 invests iff $\theta_2 > \frac{1}{2}$, which occurs with probability $\frac{3}{4}$. Thus, given that player 1 invests, the expected payoff to player 2 is 9/16.

8. Player 2 invests iff $\theta_2 > \frac{1}{2}$, which happens with probability $\frac{1}{4}$. Conditional on investing, the mean of θ_2 is $\frac{3}{4}$. Further $E[a_1 = \theta] = -\frac{1}{2}$. Hence the expected payoff to player 2 if player 1 does not invest is $\frac{1}{4}[\frac{3}{4} - \frac{1}{2}] = 1/16$.

exogenous. In this example, there is clearly an advantage to going second. Specifically, the expected return to player 1 is ¼ and the expected payoff for player 2 is ⁵⁄₁₆.

This observation brings us back to our discussion of timing and provides a basis for delay. If these agents are not forced to stagger their decisions, they would each prefer to go second and thus take advantage of the information created by the other. In this case, delay might endogenously arise.

To model this in a nontrivial fashion, we need to introduce a cost of delay into the analysis. It is convenient to discount payoffs so that the informational advantage of moving second is potentially offset by discounting. Further, we need to specify the game of timing that is used to determine the order of moves.

One possible extensive form is that the players, prior to observing the realized values of θ_i, simultaneously decide whether to go first or second. This is similar to the structure used earlier where players decided on odd or even as their period of action. Assuming that the discount factor, denoted by δ, is close enough to 1, there is still some gain to going second. However, we must consider the possibility that both players move in either the first or second period, thus denying to both the benefit of the information created by the action of the other.

First consider an equilibrium in which moves are staggered. If player 1 acts in the first period, then for δ close enough to 1, player 2 will best respond by acting in the second period. Given this, player 1's best response is to act first since there are no gains to joining player 2 and acting second. Hence, by symmetry, there are two staggered pure strategy equilibria for δ near 1. In fact, the game has a battle of the sexes structure and so there is also a mixed strategy equilibrium.

When players move simultaneously in the first period, they each have an expected payoff of ¼ since they invest iff θ_1 exceeds 0. If they move simultaneously in the second period, their expected payoff is simply $\delta/4$. In both of these cases, there are no flows of information The candidate equilibrium in which each player waits until period 2 is not an equilibrium because of discounting. However, for sufficiently low values of δ, there will be an equilibrium without delay. Otherwise, there are no equilibria with simultaneous investment.

The problem with this extensive form game is that agents must commit to the period of their move prior to observing their signal. Perhaps a more compelling model of timing is one in which the agents decide whether or not to invest after receiving their signal, θ_i. In this case, for sufficiently large values of the signal, the agent will surely invest, trading off the gain to moving early from the information conveyed by the other's choice. For very low values of the signal, it is clear too that the agent will wait, perhaps never investing for sufficiently low values of θ_i. For intermediate values of the signal, the agent will optimally wait for the other to invest and then invest in the second period iff the other invests.

For this model, Gale [1996b] constructs such an equilibrium. There is a critical value of θ, say θ^*, such that if

1. θ_i exceeds θ^* player i invests in period 1 and
2. otherwise, player i will wait and invest in period 2 iff the expected return, given that the other player invests in the first period, is positive.

Gale argues that there exists a unique value of θ^* satisfying these conditions.[9] Further, $\theta^* > 0$; the option value of waiting exceeds the slight expected gain to investing early.

A very interesting feature of this equilibrium is that the player who delays will invest iff the other agent invests in the first period. To see why, suppose that the agent's decision in the second period were independent of the action of the other. Then there would be a cost to delay but no benefit since actions are independent; this is not equilibrium behavior. Thus, in equilibrium, delay arises because the actions of one player will influence the other.

Since the equilibrium is symmetric, there is always the possibility that both players delay their investment and, in equilibrium, never invest. Further, as $\theta^* > 0$, this scenario, in which no agent undertakes investment, may arise even if this investment is, ex post, profitable for both.

This discussion is, of course, made simple by the assumption of two players and two periods. Still, the model gets across some important intuition about the nature of the complementarity created by informational linkages and the possibility of equilibria with delay. We now turn to a brief overview of Chamley and Gale [1994] for further developments of this theme.

Chamley and Gale consider a situation in which there are N players and time is discrete though the horizon is infinite, i.e., $t = 1, 2, \ldots$. Players share a common discount factor δ. Of the N players, only n of them have the option of undertaking an investment project. Further, n is a random

---

9. For a closely related economy, Chamley [1997] finds the possibility of multiple equilibria.

variable. While agents know whether they have the option on an investment project, they do not know the realized value of n. Agents with a project decide whether and when to invest. The other $N - n$ agents do nothing.

If one of the n agents with an investment option exercises that option in period t, then the lifetime utility of the agent is given by $\delta^{t-1}v(n)$. The key assumption in the Chamley–Gale model is that $v(n)$ is an increasing function of n: the more agents have an investment option, the more valuable, given the date of investment, is that activity.

To recap, some agents have investment projects. Those that do care about the total number of projects in the economy. As in the examples given earlier in this section, these agents infer the realized value of n from observing the investment activity of others.

Chamley and Gale analyze the resulting game of incomplete information in which the strategy of a representative agent is a mapping from the history of play, represented here by the number of agents investing in the past periods, to the probability of investing in the current period. Of course, agents' beliefs about the realized value of n are specified as well in a manner consistent with Bayes law.

Chamley and Gale find that there exists a unique Perfect Bayesian Equilibrium. Along the equilibrium path either some or all potential investors invest or no investment activity occurs at all. The case of partial investment just reflects randomization by agents' indifference between making their investment now or delaying. Interestingly, if there is no investment in any period, then no new information is created and thus there will be no further investment. This is termed a *collapse*. They also show that if δ is large enough, there will be delay in that agents with positive expected benefits to investment may not invest with probability 1.

Note that the Chamley and Gale model ignores the ongoing nature of economic choice. Further, there is no real sense of a business cycle here, rather just a model of delay. This is not to understate the importance of this contribution but rather to point in the direction of further development.

González [1997] takes a version of this model a step further. His model has four key features. First, the structure is an overlapping generations model in which agents live for two periods. Second, the payoffs of an agent depend on a fixed (for two periods) specific shock, a common shock and some noise. Third, agents must infer the value of their idiosyncratic shock from their payoffs: i.e., information is not perfect. Fourth, the inference process is influenced by the level of economic activity: the higher the level of activity, the more precise is information about the aggregate state. Since agents' idiosyncratic shock is fixed for their lifetime, they have an incentive in youth to take actions that create information: i.e., there are learning and experimentation in the model that interact with the aggregate level of activity. Overall, González finds that the model economy displays persistence and that cycles induced by an underlying Markov process are asymmetric. In particular, the progress of the economy out of a recession is slow because agents are unaware of the change in the aggregate state from bad to good. In contrast, during good times, a change in the state to bad is easily inferred and so downturns are rather abrupt.

Real Links

Instead of exploring the issue of timing using informational links, Gale [1995, 1996a] considers a model in which the actions of agents directly influence the returns of others. In particular, the model includes complementarity through the production process as in models we investigated in Chapter 3.

As in the information problem described, there is still incentive for delay since agents may wish to wait for others to act in order to gain a return from the actions of others. Here, though, we can see that the nature of the outcome of the interaction, and thus the prospects for delay, will depend on the exact timing relationship specified in the model. Put differently, the distinction between dynamic and contemporaneous complementarities, again described in Chapter 3, may be quite important in games of timing as well.

Consider a game with two players, two periods and a dynamic technological complementarity. A player can produce either in period 1 or in period 2. The net gain to production in period 1 is θ, a nonstochastic constant for each player. The discounted value to production in period 2 is $\delta(\theta + \gamma)$ if the other player produced in period 1 and $\delta\theta$ otherwise. So delaying production has a cost due to discounting ($\delta < 1$) and a gain measured by $\gamma > 0$, the dynamic complementarity.

As before, agents simultaneously choose when to produce. Consider first a candidate equilibrium in which both agents produce in period 1. A player will choose to defect and produce in the second period iff $\delta(\theta + \gamma) \geq \theta$, or $\delta \geq \theta/(\theta + \gamma)$. So for low values of δ and γ, there will be an equilibrium in which both players produce in the first period. But for sufficiently high values of the discount factor and the technology parameter, it is an equilibrium for agents to stagger their choices.[10] Further, this staggering is perfectly efficient: the social gains from the external production effect exceed the cost of delaying production for one period.[11]

Consider, in contrast, a setting where the interaction between agents is contemporaneous rather than lagged by one period. So, assume that the productivity of an agent is enhanced by the number of other agents producing in *that* period.[12] Further, suppose that there are $N + 1$ agents with production opportunities and two periods. Output from producing with the N others is given by $\theta + N\gamma$.

Clearly, there is an equilibrium in which all agents produce in the initial period. There is no incentive for delay if all agents produce in the first period. However, there can also be an equilibrium with delay in which all agents wait until period 2 to produce. Given that others delay, an individual agent will wait as well, as long as $\delta(\theta + N\gamma) > \theta$: i.e., the gains to defection are offset by the discounted value of the complementarity. So, we have an equilibrium with delay if the discount factor is not too low and the production complementarity is large enough. For this model, the production complementarity is, in turn, partly determined by a production function parameter and partly by the number of agents. Apparently, as the number of agents rises, delay becomes more likely. Note that here delay is inefficient.

Gale [1995] goes well beyond this overly simple structure to study these issues more formally. The theme, though, is delay in a setting with production complementarities, and the main issues concern the likelihood of delay as a function of the timing of the complementarities, the discount factor and the number of agents.

In particular, Gale assumes that there are N players, each with an investment activity which can be undertaken once. Thus, in contrast to the Chamley and Gale specification, there is no uncertainty over the number of agents with investment projects. The cost of investment is fixed at c and this discrete activity creates a stream of benefits. As earlier, denote the discount factor by δ. Further, let x_{it} be the state of player i in period t, where $x_{it} \in \{0, 1\}$ and $x_{it} = 1$ indicates investment either in or before

---

10. Clearly, it is never an equilibrium for both to wait until period 2 to produce since there is no gain to delay unless the other agent moves first. So again the timing game has the same structure of the battle of the sexes game.
11. This assumes society maximizes the discounted value of output.
12. Yet another alternative would have the interaction to anyone who had ever produced up to and including the current period.

period t. The investment decision is irreversible: if $x_{it} = 1$, then $x_{it+s} = 1$ for $s > 0$. Finally, define $x_t = \sum_i x_{it}/N$, which represents the fractions of investors up to and including period t.

Assuming that the complementarities in investment are contemporaneous, the return from investment at date t is then given by

$$\sum_{s=t}^{\infty} \delta^{s-1} u(x_s) - \delta^{t-1} c \tag{13}$$

In this expression, the investor receives a payoff of $u(x_s)$ in period s where x_s is the cumulative investment at date s. Of course this state variable evolves over time as more agents invest.[13] This is perfectly anticipated by an investor in equilibrium.

Gale assumes that $u(1)/(1 - \delta) > c$. So, c is sufficiently low that if all other agents invest, the remaining agent will do so. Further, Gale assumes that $u(0)/(1 - \delta) < c$ so that an individual will not invest alone if others never invest. Finally, we assume that $u(x)$ is an increasing function, implying the presence of strategic complementarities. Thus there will exist a critical value of x, denoted x^*, such that $u(x^*)/(1 - \delta) = c$. So, at $x = x^*$, all players will invest without delay.

A static version of this model is quite close to the models of participation complementarities presented at the start of Chapter 5. Here, though, the dynamics alter the outcome and permit a study of delay. In fact, as in the simpler production complementarity economy presented earlier, it is quite easy to generate equilibria with delay.

For example, consider an equilibrium in which all players delay their investment by one period so that $x_{i1} = 0$ and $x_{i2} = 1$ for all i. Would an agent defect and invest earlier? The gain would be to enjoy an extra period of payoff from acting before the others of $u(1/N)$. The cost of moving early is that the entry cost of c is borne one period earlier. So, if $u(1/N) < (1 - \delta)c$, there will be an equilibrium with delay of one period. So, given $u(\cdot)$, delay requires a relatively small value for the discount factor and a relatively large number of players so that $1/N < x^*$.

Using this same logic it is possible to construct equilibria with even further delay as long as the gain to investing alone, $u(1/N)$, is not too large relative to the cost of incurring the entry fee earlier. In constructing these equilibria, care must be taken to describe the equilibrium strategies off the equilibrium path completely. To construct an equilibrium with two

13. Yet another version of the model might fix x_s at the time of investment.

periods of delay, we suppose that any deviations will be "ignored" in equilibrium: investment takes place in period 3 even if there is a deviation in either period 1 or period 2. To check that this is an equilibrium strategy, it must be the case that a deviation in, say, period 1 will not lead others to invest in period 2. It is straightforward to show that if $u(2/N) < (1 - \delta)c$, investment in the first period will not lead to investment in the second. Since $u(x)$ is increasing, this condition implies the previous one for an equilibrium with one-period delay. In fact, if there is no investment in the first period, then the continuation of the game is identical to the equilibrium with one period of delay described earlier.

Gale uses the recursive nature of the equilibria to prove some results on the importance of the discount factor and the number of players. First, as the period length gets arbitrarily small, so that δ becomes large, the amount of delay, in terms of the period of inactivity, is trivial. As the length of the time period becomes small, all equilibria are approximately efficient.

Second, as the number of players increases, delay becomes more likely. In fact, Gale shows that there exists a subgame Perfect Nash Equilibrium in which all players invest at date n^*, where n^* is the smallest integer greater than Nx^*. As the number of players increases, so does n^* and hence the length of delay in this particular equilibrium.

Gale also explores the case of lagging complementarities where the previous investment activity of others influences current payoffs. Again there is a cost here to the first mover and delay can arise.

SUMMARY

The point of this chapter was to explore issues of timing. Given the importance of large expenditures on producer and consumer durables for aggregate fluctuations, understanding the timing of these decisions is quite useful. In some cases, these discrete choices at the individual level will be washed away through aggregation. This seems more likely when these discrete decisions are staggered. In contrast, synchronization implies that many agents' adjusting at the microlevel will imply large aggregate movements.

The theme of this chapter is that the nature of strategic interactions will influence the timing of these actions. In particular, in large macroeconomic settings where agents are small, strategic complementarity implies synchronization of discrete activities. Though not emphasized here, it is also the case that common shocks to the payoffs of agents will have the same influence. Moreover, the discussion has highlighted the possibility of delay arising from the interaction between agents.

Except for relatively few studies, the macroeconomic implications of these timing issues have not been fully studied. In particular, the empirical studies of discrete choices generally allow for common disturbances but, for tractability, ignore strategic interactions. As always, distinguishing shocks from these interactions will be critical in any empirical implementation of these models.

7   Government Policy

In this final section of the book we are interested in studying the problem of policy determination between a government and a set of private agents.[1] The inefficiencies created by the presence of external effects as well as the prospects of multiple equilibria studied in the previous chapter set the stage for a consideration of government intervention to resolve these problems. Thus this topic is a natural conclusion to our study of macroeconomic complementarities.

The starting point of the chapter is an illustration of the coordinating power of the government. If coordination problems reflect the inability of agents to select the Pareto-optimal (optimistic) Nash equilibrium, then the government may be able to take actions to achieve the desired outcome. As we shall see, the government's actions can eliminate some undesirable equilibria by turning the strategies that support them into dominated strategies. These policies can be thought of as "confidence building measures" that work by eliminating the pessimistic beliefs that support the Pareto-inferior (pessimistic) Nash equilibria.

One important theme here is that *in the optimistic equilibrium*, the government never takes an action. Instead, its commitment to an action is sufficient for stabilization through removal of the pessimistic equilibrium. Thus governments may appear to be doing "nothing" when, in fact, they are quite successful.

To illustrate, we study the Diamond and Dybvig [1983] model of bank

---

1. Discussions with Hubert Kempf about the structure and content of this chapter were greatly appreciated.

runs and the role of the government in supporting the Pareto optimal equilibrium through the creation of deposit insurance. For this example, the government's promise to pay deposit insurance eliminates bank runs by making the early withdrawal of deposits (the strategy that supports the pessimistic equilibrium) a dominated strategy.

The second section of the chapter provides a contrasting perspective of the government. In particular, we study situations in which the government is a destabilizing influence as it creates rather than resolves strategic uncertainty. Thus this discussion introduces a new source of complementarity through government policy.

The final section of the chapter takes up the important topic of commitment and the associated theme of time consistency. While this well-known literature certainly has its origins outside the models of strategic complementarity and multiple equilibria that form the core of this book, there are numerous important connections between them.

First, the inability to commit to action is a powerful constraint on the coordinating role of the government. Even in the context of the Diamond–Dybvig model in which the government's creation of deposit insurance appears to resolve the coordination problem, it is assumed that the government can commit to taking the actions necessary to prevent bank runs. If this commitment is not present, it is no longer apparent that the government's stabilizing role remains. In fact, as we shall discuss, the destabilizing role of the government can be related to its inability to commit to certain policies.

Second, the time consistency literature requires a "tension" between the interests of the government and those of private agents. A critical theoretical issue is understanding and evaluating the basis for this tension. Using the framework created by Chari, Kehoe and Prescott [1989], we focus on two elements: (i) differences in tastes between the government and private agents and (ii) the presence of externalities that create inefficiencies in the private economy. It is when we consider the effects of externalities that we return to many themes in the literature on macroeconomic complementarities.

The presentation of this material begins with the framework of Chari, Kehoe and Prescott. This general structure is then used to study some examples: the theory of inflation (as in Kydland and Prescott [1977] and Barro and Gordon [1983]), the determination of capital income taxes (as in Fischer [1980]) and the effects of government subsidies in an economy with production complementarities.

THE GOVERNMENT AS A SOURCE
OF CONFIDENCE

The existence of multiple, Pareto-ranked equilibria motivates government intervention to eliminate the Pareto-inferior equilibria and thus support the Pareto-superior equilibrium. In fact, the government may attempt to use its powers further and thus achieve allocations that dominate even the best equilibrium. But here we focus on public confidence building measures that steer the economy away from the pitfalls of pessimism. In some cases, along the equilibrium path active government intervention will not be needed: a credible promise to act is sufficient. Still, the policy must be credible so that agents believe that the government will live up to its promises.

A leading example of this form of government intervention arises in the design of deposit insurance to prevent bank runs. The starting point is a model of multiple equilibria in the banking system which is broadly consistent with the bank runs observed in the United States prior to the introduction of deposit insurance in the mid-1930s. While the banking system in the United States has since had financial problems, bank failures have dramatically decreased since the introduction of deposit insurance. Note that if this insurance is successful, no payments are needed. Again, the power of the policy arises from a commitment by the government to take an action in the event of a bank run.

Using the well-known model of Diamond and Dybvig [1983], we know that uncertain, private liquidity needs by depositors can lead to instability in the process of intermediation. In one equilibrium, lenders without current liquidity needs leave their funds with an intermediary and only those lenders with current needs withdraw funds. In a second equilibrium, all lenders, regardless of their liquidity needs, attempt to withdraw funds from the intermediary. Diamond and Dybvig show that this second equilibrium, a bank run, exists as long as the commitment of the intermediary to early withdrawers is large relative to the liquid resources available to the intermediary.

To be more complete, consider an economy that lasts for three periods. There is a large number of agents (N) at the start of time, period 1. Each agent has an endowment of 1 unit of the single good in youth and can live at most two more periods. With probability π, an agent will live for only two periods and thus, by assumption, consume only in period 2. These agents are termed *early consumers*. With probability $(1 - \pi)$, an agent is a late consumer and, again by assumption, consumes only in period 3. Agents learn their type at the start of period 2 and this may be private information.

There is a simple institution, an intermediary, in this economy that facilitates the transfer of resources over time. The intermediary offers agents deposit contacts that provide for period 2 and period 3 consumption, (c_2) and (c_3), per unit goods deposited in period 1. The intermediary has access to a linear technology that uses goods in period 1 as inputs. The technology can deliver either 1 unit of the good in period 2 or $R > 1$ units in period 3, per unit deposited.[2] We also assume that agents have access to a private technology that allows them to store (with a zero net return) goods over time.

If agent types were observable, then the intermediary would offer a contract in period 1 to maximize

$$\pi u(c_2) + (1 - \pi)u(c_3) \tag{1}$$

subject to a breakeven constraint that

$$(1 - \pi)c_3 = (1 - \pi c_2)R \tag{2}$$

where the period utility function $u(c)$ is assumed to be strictly increasing and strictly concave. The breakeven constraint (2) says that the late consumers receive the return of R times the amount of the original deposit not paid to the early consumers. In this way, the bank offers an optimal contract that provides insurance to agents across their types and provides some liquidity to the early consumers.

The optimal contract satisfies the breakdown constraint and the first-order condition of

$$u'(c_2) = Ru'(c_3) \tag{3}$$

Since $R > 1$ and $u(c)$ is strictly concave, $c_3 > c_2$. If $u(c) = \ln(c)$, then the optimal contract will satisfy $c_2 = 1$ and $c_3 = R$. If $u(c)$ has more curvature than the natural log function, then $c_2 > 1$ and $c_3 < R$. Essentially the extra curvature implies that the consumers receive more insurance and thus a "flatter" consumption profile.

If agent types are not observable, then the deposit contract must be incentive compatible and feasible. Without delving into the problem of

---

2. See Cooper–Ross [1998] and the references therein for a discussion of alternative models of the intermediation process, particularly the specification of the intertemporal technology.

finding an optimal contract, it is useful to see whether the full information contract is incentive compatible.

One equilibrium is for agents to reveal their types truthfully.[3] Clearly, early consumers have no incentive to misrepresent their taste types since they do not value consumption in period 3. If all later consumers announce their true type, than a remaining late consumer will be honest as well since $c_2 < c_3$ and storage yields a zero net return.[4] So, neither type has an incentive to be dishonest *if* others are truthful.

Interestingly, there is another equilibrium if $c_2 > 1$. In this case, if all agents claim to be early consumers, then the intermediary simply does not have the resources to pay all agents, both early and later consumers, the consumption level c_2. To see the construction of this equilibrium, it is necessary to demonstrate that if all other agents, both early and late consumers, claim to be early consumers, then a remaining agent ought to claim to be an early consumer as well. If this remaining agent is an early consumer, there is clearly no benefit to misrepresenting, as argued before. Further, if this remaining agent is a later consumer, then this agent is also better off claiming to be an early consumer in hopes of being lucky enough to obtain c_2 from the bank and using the storage technology to finance late consumption. Given that the bank does not have sufficient resources to meet the withdrawals of all the depositors, the late consumer is sure to receive nothing by telling the truth.[5] This second equilibrium is the bank run described earlier.

When there are multiple equilibria of this type, there is a simple policy for the government which eliminates the bank run. Under this policy, the government promises to pay funds to all agents who are unable to withdraw deposits from the intermediary. When this policy is in force, depositors without current liquidity needs have no incentive to withdraw their funds regardless of the behavior of other late consumers. So, the policy converts truth telling into a dominant strategy and thus the bank runs equilibrium is eliminated. Note that in equilibrium the government is never called upon to provide insurance. Of course, the government policy of providing

---

3. Here we are adopting the language of the mechanism design literature, where agents announce their types.
4. So, a late consumer acting as an early consumer would withdraw c_2 and store it for one period, thus consuming less than c_3.
5. Here we are assuming that the bank cannot limit the withdrawals of the agents through a suspension of convertibility. Diamond–Dybvig show that if there is aggregate uncertainty over the fraction of early consumers, the suspension of convertibility will not be enough to prevent a bank run.

this insurance must be credible: that is, it must have a tax base to raise the funds to pay the depositors in the event of a run and a will to do so if needed.

In fact, this example is just the tip of the iceberg. There are numerous examples of government guarantees that are presumably established to overcome crises of confidence.[6] A recent example is the intervention of the U.S. government in Mexico, where a financial guarantee was established to restore confidence of lenders.[7]

THE GOVERNMENT AS A SOURCE OF MULTIPLE EQUILIBRIA

The following example highlights the stabilizing role of the government. Here a well intentioned government, committed to the bolstering of confidence, takes actions to support a Pareto-dominant equilibrium. To do so, it is necessary that the government have the interests of the agents as its objective and also have the ability to commit. We return later to discussing the consequences of alternative assumptions about the government's objectives and its commitment powers.

Another point that is hidden in the Diamond–Dybvig example is the nature of the government's ability to raise revenues to provide the deposit insurance. If, for example, the government raises its revenue through some form of distortionary taxes, then its taxation policies can by themselves create multiple equilibria.[8] This is because the tax rates can become endogenous variables and thus depend on "the actions of others." In this manner, we shall see that the government can indeed create rather than eliminate strategic uncertainty. To make this point, we consider the taxation policies of the government in isolation.

As a simple but illuminating example of this, consider a static economy consisting of a large number of agents and a government.[9] Suppose that agents put forth work effort (n) to maximize utility where consumption (c) is financed from labor income once the government has taxed at a rate of τ. Let $u(c, n)$ represent the utility of a representative agent where the

---

6. Cooper–Ross [1997b] provide a framework for discussing a wide range of guaranty funds, both public and private, that serve to bolster confidence.
7. See Obstfeld [1996] for a discussion of currency crises in a model with complementarities.
8. Cooper–Ross [1997b] raise a similar point in discussing the strategic uncertainty created by the design of private guarantee funds.
9. The point of this example is also made by Eaton [1987] and by Persson and Tabellini [1990].

budget constraint is $c = (1 - \tau)n$.[10] The agent takes the tax rate as given, and optimal behavior leads to a labor supply of $n^*(\tau)$, suppressing the wage rate in the notation. Assume that labor supply is increasing in the real after-tax wage, so that $n^*(\tau)$ is a decreasing function.

The government has a budget balance constraint that total tax revenues must finance its fixed per capita budget expenditures, G. Letting $N(\tau)$ equal the average supply of labor in the economy, budget balance implies that $\tau = G/N(\tau)$. Substituting this into the labor supply decision of an individual, we find $n = n^*(G/N)$. Thus the budget balance condition creates a link across agents. In fact, there is a complementarity at work here: if others work more, the tax rate will fall, inducing the remaining agent to work more as well.

With this insight, it is not difficult to construct examples of multiple equilibria in this static tax problem. It is sufficient to search for tax rates that satisfy the condition of $\tau = G/N(\tau)$. Note that this version of the budget balance condition incorporates both individual optimization and the fact that all agents are identical since $N(\tau)$ is the common level of labor supply given the tax rate.

For example, assume that $u(c, n) = c - \frac{1}{2}n^{\frac{1}{2}}$ so that labor supply is given by $n = (1 - \tau)$. Hence the condition for an equilibrium tax rate is simply

$$\tau(1 - \tau) = G \qquad\qquad\qquad (4)$$

Any value of the tax rate that satisfies (4) is an equilibrium. As long as $G < \frac{1}{4}$, there will be two solutions to (4). One solution will entail a high tax rate and low employment, while the other will have a low tax rate and therefore a high level of employment. In equilibrium, the utility of a representative agent is given by $\frac{1}{2}(1 - \tau)^2$ so that the low tax equilibrium is Pareto-dominant.

Note that this multiplicity arises in the simultaneous game between the government and the private agents. If the government moves before private agents and sets the tax rate, then it will select the Pareto-dominant, low tax rate equilibrium.

A similar theme appears in the work of Schmitt-Grohe and Uribe [1996], who study the behavior of the stochastic growth model with a government budget constraint.[11] They investigate an economy in which the government raises revenue, as in the preceding example, with a distortionary tax on

---

10. Implicitly there is a real wage of 1.
11. See also Guo and Lansing [1997].

labor income. As the economy is dynamic, future taxes as well as current ones influence the choices of agents. Assuming that labor supply is infinitely elastic, they prove that the steady state equilibrium of their model may be indeterminate.

In their economy, a representative agent works and rents capital to competitive firms. The individual pays a tax on labor earnings and then splits income between consumption and savings, through the accumulation of capital. Thus the model is based upon the standard stochastic growth model. Preferences are assumed to be separable between consumption and leisure, and labor supply is perfectly elastic.

The action, as in the preceding static example of multiple equilibria with government taxation of labor income, comes from the interaction of the government and the private agents. Initially, they assume that the government taxes labor income only. The government finances a fixed level of expenditures from the labor income tax. The government budget constraint is given by

$$G = \tau_t w_t H_t \tag{5}$$

where τ_t is the tax rate, w_t is the equilibrium wage before taxes and H_t is hours worked by the representative agent. Note that labor demand by the firm will set the wage equal to the marginal product of capital, and thus the level of the capital stock will enter into the relationship between taxes and the labor input. Each agent takes this tax rate as given when optimizing, though the tax rate must be determined as part of the overall equilibrium.

Schmitt-Grohe and Uribe analyze a continuous time economy and focus on the dynamics in the neighborhood of a steady state. The economy is reduced to two dynamic equations with the capital stock and the marginal utility of consumption as state variables. As in the analysis of the production complementarity models in Chapter 3, the key is the local stability of the steady state. Since the model is cast in continuous time, the condition for sunspot equilibria is that both eigenvalues of the system are negative.

Schmitt-Grohe and Uribe argue that the steady state is indeterminate iff the tax rate on labor income lies between capital's share, a parameter of the Cobb–Douglas technology, and the tax rate that maximizes government revenue, i.e., the tax rate at the peak of the Laffer curve. The authors argue that these are not unreasonable conditions given that capital's share is less than 40%.

In this model, the indeterminacy again rests upon labor supply's being flatter than an upward sloping labor demand. By assumption, labor supply is completely elastic. Schmitt-Grohe and Uribe argue that in equilibrium (i.e., after substituting out for the tax rate), there is a positive relationship between the log deviation of the after tax wage rate from its steady state and the log deviation of hours worked iff the tax rate exceeds capital's share.

Put differently, higher tax rates anticipated for the future imply a decreased desire for the accumulation of capital. This implies that output in the current period is lower and thus taxes today must be higher as well. Alternatively, expectations of low taxes tomorrow can be self-fulfilling as well, and thus an intertemporal complementarity is present.

A GENERAL STRUCTURE FOR COMMITMENT PROBLEMS

The discussion thus far has highlighted the interactions of the government with the theme of multiple equilibria. In particular, one example illustrates the government's role in coordinating the economy, and the other illustrates the possibility that the government may create strategic uncertainty.

In the discussion of the government as a coordinator, we noted that it was critical that the government's promise to take action was credible. One way to have credibility is to have the ability to commit to an action. Further, in order for the government with commitment to adopt the policy of deposit insurance, it was necessary that the government share the interest of private agents in resolving the coordination problem. Thus in order to stabilize, the government must have the interests of private agents as its objective and must have the power of commitment.

In the discussion of the government as a destabilizing influence, the issue of commitment arose again. If the government were able to move first, then its taxation policies would not create any coordination problems. The government created strategic uncertainty because agents had to forecast its policy variable.

This section of the chapter takes up this fairly broad topic of commitment and government objectives. There is a vast literature under the heading of "political economy" in which the design of government policy, in terms of both objectives and constraints, is studied.[12] Our more narrow focus here will be on the issue of commitment and the related topic of time

---

12. For a presentation of this material, Persson and Tabellini [1994] provide an extended set of articles.

consistency in the context of economies with externalities; we draw heavily upon Chari, Kehoe and Prescott [1989] to develop a general representation of the interactions between a government and a group of private agents.

In particular, we focus on the nature of a conflict between the agents that leads to what has been termed a *time consistency problem*. Informally, the idea is to take as a benchmark the equilibrium allocation that would arise when the government takes actions before private agents. This is often termed the *solution with (government) commitment*. Now, take the actions chosen by the private agents as given and allow the government to reoptimize. The critical question is, Will the government choose an action different from that in the equilibrium where the government moved first?

If the answer is "yes," so that government chooses to act differently, then there is a time consistency problem associated with the equilibrium of the game in which the government moves first. This does not invalidate the commitment solution. If the government has the ability to commit, then the equilibrium computed for that extensive form game is certainly the predicted outcome. But the time inconsistency of the commitment solution does point to the fact that if the government can in some way renege on its "move," then it will want to do so.

As we shall see, the time consistency problem revolves around two themes. In some cases, the time consistency problem arises simply as a result of differences in objectives between private agents and the government. In other envrironments, the problem results from the presence of externalities that are not internalized by the private agents. The existence of these externalities creates both a rationale for government intervention and the basis for the time consistency problem.

From the perspective of macroeconomics, the study of the problem of policy credibility (sometimes termed *time consistency*) has led to positive theories of inflation (Kydland and Prescott [1977]) and taxation (e.g., Fischer [1980]). We take up these leading examples at the end of this subsection. In addition, we consider an example built upon a model of production complementarities.

The Role of Conflict and Externalities in the Time Consistency Problem

To fix notation and some basic ideas, consider the interaction between a large group of private agents and a government. Each private agent controls *x* and the government controls the policy variable π. Suppose that the preferences of the agents and the government are given by $U(x, \pi)$. So, by assumption, there is no conflict whatsoever between the government and the private agent.

Further, the payoff to each agent depends only on the action of that agent and the action of the government. So, there are absolutely no interactions between the private agents. Since agents are identical, it is sufficient to consider the interaction between a single (representative) private agent and the government.

As this section proceeds, we will allow for differences in objectives and interactions across agents. For now, think of this model as a useful building block.

In this example, one can generally consider four allocations. They differ in terms of the nature of interaction between the agents and the government (cooperative vs. noncooperative games) and in the order of moves in the noncooperative games. Throughout this analysis we assume that there is a unique equilibrium for each of these extensive forms.[13]

The first, which we will term the *cooperative solution*, involves the optimization of $U(x, \pi)$ jointly by the government and the representative agent. The term *cooperative solution* is used since the government and the agent jointly agree and commit to the choice of (x, π): there is no possibility of deviations from the agreed upon actions. This serves as a benchmark for the noncooperative equilibria since, by construction, this solution yields the highest payoff to the agents. The other three allocations refer to outcomes under different timing assumptions for the noncooperative game played between the government and the representative agent.

The second allocation is the *simultaneous move solution*. In this case, all agents and the government move simultaneously, taking the actions of others as given. Let $\phi(x)$ denote the best response of the government to the strategy *x* chosen by each representative agent and let $\psi(\pi)$ denote the best response of a representative agent to the choice of the government. Hence an equilibrium for the simultaneous move game is a pair (x^{**}, π^{**}) with the property that $x^{**} = \psi(\pi^{**})$ and $\pi^{**} = \phi(x^{**})$, the usual mutual best response property.

The third allocation is termed the *commitment solution*. By this, we mean the outcome of a noncooperative game in which the government

---

13. So at this point we are forced to eliminate the possibility of multiple equilibria from consideration though externalities remain a key element.

moves first: i.e., it can commit to the choice of policy (π) prior to the choice of x by the agent. In selecting its policy, the government anticipates the response of the private agents, given by the reaction function $\psi(\pi)$. So, the commitment solution is a pair (x^*, π^*) such that π^* maximizes $U(\psi(\pi), \pi)$. Of course, the use of the term *commitment* to describe this game assumes the perspective of the government.

The final allocation is termed the *no-commitment solution*. In this case, it is the private agent that moves first and the government that follows. Here, though, we make use of the fact that there are many private agents. So each assumes the action of the government is independent of his/her action: i.e., private agents act independently and take the (anticipated) government's policy as given. Hence, the simultaneous move and no-commitment solutions are identical. So, we will ignore this solution.

Using this notation, we can restate the point of time consistency. Generally, we will be asking the following question to determine whether the commitment solution is time consistent: Taking the action of the private agent in the commitment solution as given (x^*), what is the government's best response? If this is *not* the same as the government action taken in the commitment solution, then a time consistency problem exists. So, if $\pi^* \neq \phi(x^*)$, then a time consistency problem exists.

The relationship between these solutions and the time consistency problem is summarized in the following:

> **Proposition 1:** *The commitment and simultaneous move solutions differ iff there is a time consistency problem.*
>
> **Proof:** To see why, recall our assumption that there is a unique equilibrium for these games. We first show that if the solutions differ, then there is a time consistency problem: i.e., if $(x^*, \pi^*) \neq (x^{**}, \pi^{**})$, then $\pi^* \neq \phi(x^*)$. Suppose not, so that $\pi^* = \phi(x^*)$. If so, then (x^*, π^*) would be a Nash equilibrium of the simultaneous game since in the commitment solution $x^* = \psi(\pi^*)$. This contradicts the hypothesis that $(x^*, \pi^*) \neq (x^{**}, \pi^{**})$ given our uniqueness assumption.
>
> We now show that if there is a time consistency problem, then the solutions must differ: i.e., if $\pi^* \neq \phi(x^*)$, then $(x^*, \pi^*) \neq (x^{**}, \pi^{**})$. Suppose not, so that $(x^*, \pi^*) = (x^{**}, \pi^{**})$: i.e., the commitment solution is the Nash equilibrium of the simultaneous move game. However, this requires $\pi^* = \phi(x^*)$ and thus contradicts the hypothesis.
>
> QED.

So, to determine whether or not the commitment solution is time consistent, we will simply look for differences between that solution and the simultaneous move solution. Further, since the simultaneous move solution and the one in which the government moves after private agents are identical, knowing that the commitment and simultaneous move solutions differ implies that the government would want to change its decision if it moves after the private agents.

In the simple example of the representative private agent and a benevolent government, there is no time consistency problem. In fact, it should be clear that all four solutions are identical since the government and the private agent have exactly the same objective.

To see this, note first that the allocation from the cooperative solution satisfies the conditions

$$U_\pi(x, \pi) = U_x(x, \pi) = 0 \qquad (6)$$

This is obtained from directly choosing (x, π) to maximize $U(x, \pi)$.

In the commitment solution, the government chooses π given the choice of agents that it anticipates, denoted by $\psi(\pi)$. Thus the government solves $\max_\pi U(\psi(\pi), \pi)$, leading to a first-order condition of

$$U_x(x, \pi)\psi_\pi + U_\pi(x, \pi) = 0 \qquad (7)$$

where ψ_π is the derivative of the optimal response of the private agent to π. Since individual optimization, given π, leads to $U_x(x, \pi) = 0$, it is clear that the cooperative solution is also the equilibrium of the game with commitment.

For the simultaneous move game, the conditions for equilibrium are exactly those from the cooperative solution given in (6). In fact the two conditions given in (6) are those that characterize the mutual best response properties necessary for a Nash equilibrium of the simultaneous move game.

So the equilibria under all four concepts are the same. In particular, this means that the solution with commitment is time consistent: even if the government could move after private agents, it has no incentive to change its action relative to the commitment solution. Formally, this is seen by the fact that the commitment and simultaneous move outcomes are the same.

The result that there is no time consistency problem stems partly from the fact that without a difference in objectives between the government and the agents, the government has no reason to use the first-mover advantage it is granted in the commitment solution. Likewise, since there is no source of inefficiency in the interaction between private agents, there is no reason for the government to use its power to influence the actions of the private agents. Clearly, then, the origins of the problem must lie with differences in objectives or, perhaps more interestingly, in the interaction of agents in a multiple agent economy.

To study the case of divergent interests, suppose that the government has an objective other than the maximization of $U(x, \pi)$, say, $V(x, \pi)$, perhaps reflecting the private objectives of the bureaucrats. In this case, the commitment solution and the simultaneous move solution will surely differ.

With commitment, the government will use its first-mover advantage to attempt to influence the choice of x by the private agent. This leads to the following set of first-order conditions

$$U_x(x, \pi) = 0 \tag{8}$$
$$V_x(x, \pi)\psi_\pi + V_\pi(x, \pi) = 0$$

where again ψ_π is the derivative of the optimal response of the private agent to π.

In the simultaneous move case, the influence of π on x is gone as the government takes the action of the representative agent as given. The equilibrium to this game satisfies

$$U_x(x, \pi) = 0, \qquad V_\pi(x, \pi) = 0 \tag{9}$$

As long as there is some form of interaction between the government and the private sector (so that ψ_π is not 0) the solutions to these two systems of first-order conditions will not be the same.

So, generally if there is a divergence in interests between the government and the private agents, then the timing of moves of the extensive form game matters. That is, there is a time consistency problem associated with the commitment solution. Intuitively, the government initially chose an action to meet it own objectives and to influence the choice of the agent, as in (8). However, once x is chosen, the government cannot influence the agent and thus wants to take a different action.

Interestingly enough, the time consistency problem can arise when there is no divergence of interests between the government and the private sector. This requires the specification of an economy with multiple private sector agents along with a source of inefficiency in their interaction.

To illustrate this, Chari, Kehoe and Prescott present a single model of interaction between agents, not unlike many of the models with externalities and complementarities explored in earlier chapters of this book. Suppose that there are I agents index $i = 1, 2, \ldots I$ where the payoff to i is given by $U(x_i, X, \pi)$. In this payoff function, X represents the mean value of x over the agents. As before, π is the action of the government. The government's objective is to maximize $\Sigma_i U(x_i, X, \pi)$. In a symmetric equilibrium in the game between private agents, $x_i = X$ so that the government is again maximizing the objective of a representative agent.

In the commitment solution, the private agents play a game given π since their payoffs depend on the actions of others through X. Since the payoff functions are the same for all players, we focus on symmetric Nash equilibria given π and assume that a unique equilibrium exists. Denote the equilibrium by $x^*(\pi)$ given implicitly by

$$U_x(x^*(\pi), x^*(\pi), \pi) = 0 \tag{10}$$

Given $x^*(\pi)$, the government selects π to maximize $\Sigma_i U(x_i, X, \pi)$ with $x = X = x^*(\pi)$. The first-order condition for the government's problem, using the agent's first-order condition to delete a term, is

$$U_X(x, x, \pi)\frac{\partial\, x^*(\pi)}{\partial\, \pi} + U_\pi(x, x, \pi) = 0 \tag{11}$$

These derivatives are all evaluated at $x = x^*(\pi)$.

In the simultaneous move solution, the optimal choice of government policy satisfies

$$U_\pi(x, x, \pi) = 0 \tag{12}$$

assuming, as before, that the outcome of the interaction of the agents will be a symmetric equilibrium in which all agents choose the same level of x. Since each agent takes the actions of other agents and the government as given, the first-order condition for a representative agent at the equilibrium is

$$U_x(x, x, \pi) = 0 \tag{13}$$

The commitment solution, (10)–(11), and the simultaneous move solution, (12)–(13), are clearly different. The time consistency problem arises from the fact that with commitment the government has the ability to influence the choice of the private agents while without commitment, this opportunity is gone. Note, though, that if there were no externality, so that $U_x(x, X, \pi)$ were always equal to 0, then the time consistency problem would disappear. Of course, in that case, we would simply be back to the world of multiple agents without any conflict.

Some Leading Examples

Here we discuss three leading examples of the policy credibility problem. Much of the literature on policy games in macroeconomics builds upon the first two examples. We also offer a third example, which discusses the role of government intervention in an economy with complementarities in the production process.

A Positive Theory of Inflation

As in Kydland and Prescott [1977] and Barro and Gordon [1983], consider an economy composed of a government and many private agents. The government, or monetary authorities, through their control of the money supply, are assumed to control the actual rate of inflation. The objective of the monetary authority is to minimize

$$A(N_t - N^*)^2 + (\pi_t)^2 \tag{14}$$

where N^* is the desired level of employment from the perspective of the monetary authorities. In what follows, we consider N^* to be the efficient level of employment in the economy. Note that the monetary authority is assumed to incur losses from variations of employment around the target and from inflation differing from zero.

As a convenient short-cut, we view (private) agent i as choosing π^e_{it}, the expected rate of inflation in the economy. All private agents incur losses from deviations of actual inflation from their expectations. That is, the payoff to agent i is simply $(\pi^e_{it} - \pi_t)^2$.

One should think of this as an economy in which there are many private agents all attempting to forecast inflation in order to make employment decisions. Alternatively, one can imagine an economy in which wages reflect anticipated inflation and employment is determined ex post, reflecting actual inflation. In this case, private agents might again, through a reduced form, have preferences over the gap between actual and expected inflation. The economywide expected rate of inflation (π^e_t) is then the average of the expected inflation rates of the individuals in the economy.

Without being specific at all about the microeconomic structure of this economy, suppose that the aggregate level of employment in the economy depends on both the actual and the expected rates of inflation and is given by

$$N_t = N_n + \gamma (\pi_t - \pi^e_t) \tag{15}$$

Assuming that $\gamma > 0$, employment expands beyond the natural rate (N_n) when the actual rate of inflation (π_t) exceeds that expected on average by the private agents in the economy (π^e_t).

In terms of the discussion, a key issue in this example is the nature of the extensive form. In particular, does the government move before, simultaneously with or after the private agents? Does the timing matter for the outcome and for the welfare of the agents in this economy?

First, suppose that the government chooses the rate of inflation prior to the choice of private agents. That is, the government commits to an inflation rate and then the private agents take actions (summarized by π^e_t) given the action of the government. Since private agents have the same objective, they would all set their expected inflation levels equal to the inflation rate selected by the government. From (15), this implies that $N_t = N_n$ regardless of the level of inflation selected by the government. Knowing this, the optimal choice of inflation for the government is zero, thus minimizing the loss from inflation. This yields an outcome of zero inflation and a level of employment at the natural rate and is the commitment solution.

Given this solution, would the government wish to revise its choice of inflation policy? That is, once private agents act on an expectation of zero inflation, would the government wish to alter the actual rate of inflation? To answer this, consider the best response of the government in its choice of inflation to a given level of expected inflation by private agents. Call this the best response function $\phi(\pi^e)$,[14] which is given by

$$\phi(\pi^e_t) = \alpha(N^* - N_n) + \gamma\alpha\pi^e_t \tag{16}$$

where

$$\alpha \equiv \frac{A\gamma}{(1 + A\gamma^2)}$$

From this, we see that at $\pi^e_t = 0$, $\pi_t > (<) \ 0$ as $N^* > (<) N_n$. So if the natural rate of employment is lower than the government's target, then the government has an incentive to create inflation when the private sector expects zero inflation. In the presence of externalities in the labor market associated with search and production activities, it might be that the natural rate of employment is too low relative to the efficient level, as is generally assumed in this literature.

The fact that the government would prefer to change its action once

---

14. This expression is just the first-order condition for the government's choice of π given the common inflation expectation of the agents.

private agents have moved implies that the solution with commitment is not *time consistent*. Of course, this does not tell us what the outcome of the analysis is in the event that the government is unable to commit since agents, moving prior to the government, will perfectly anticipate the government's reaction given in (16).

Suppose then that the government and private agents move simultaneously. In this case, the Nash equilibrium is given by the joint solution of two equations: the best response function of the government, given in (16), and the best response function of the representative agent, $\pi^e_t = \pi_t$. The level of inflation in the Nash equilibrium is therefore given by

$$\pi^* = \frac{\alpha(N^* - N_n)}{(1 - \alpha\gamma)} \tag{17}$$

where $\alpha\gamma < 1$. So, as long as the natural rate of employment is inefficiently low, there is positive inflation in the Nash equilibrium of this game. Note that this inflation is perfectly understood by the private agents so that employment remains at N_n and there is simply a cost to society of positive inflation. Nonetheless, an outcome with zero inflation is unattainable since the government has an incentive to inflate when private agents anticipate zero inflation.

The outcome of the game in which the government moves after the private agents is exactly the same as the outcome of the simultaneous move game. If all private agents set their expected inflation at π^*, then the government has an incentive to choose exactly this level of inflation.

Overall, this example highlights a few important themes in this literature. First, the order of moves does matter in terms of the outcome of these policy games. Generally, we find that the outcome with government commitment is not time consistent. Second, there is a welfare loss from the inability to commit. In this inflation example, this is seen from the fact that the outcome of the simultaneous move game has positive inflation but the same level of employment as in the outcome with government commitment.

The example can be reinterpreted to highlight the issue of the objectives of the players and the basis for conflict discussed in the context of the Chari, Kehoe and Prescott formulation. The inflation example rests on the inefficiency of the outcome in the private economy, which provides a tradeoff for the policymaker between the costs and benefits of surprise inflation. In the absence of this inefficiency, there would be no gains to surprise inflation and hence no time consistency problem. However, the preceding formulation of the problem, though traditional, actually obscures the true source of the time consistency problem since the inefficiency in the interaction of the private agents is too implicit.

Chari, Kehoe and Prescott provide a more explicit model. Let the payoff to agent i, $i = 1, 2, \ldots I$, be given by

$$U_i = U(w_i - \pi, w - \pi, \pi) \tag{18}$$

In this payoff function, the first argument is the difference between the wage growth set by agent i (w_i) and the inflation rate, π. The second argument is the difference between the economywide average wage growth ($w \equiv \Sigma_i w_i / I$) and the inflation rate. This second argument is critical in the inflation example, though the basis for its inclusion is not clear. Finally, it is assumed that individuals' payoffs depend on the rate of inflation directly as well.

In the earlier discussion of the inflation example, we focused solely on the first of these three arguments. Since agents take w and π as given once I is large enough, only the first argument is relevant for decision making at the level of the individual. However, these other arguments of payoffs are quite important when we consider the choice of the policymaker.

In that regard, let the payoffs of the government be given by $\Sigma_i U_i$. In fact, using these objectives, one can go through the steps of characterizing the conditions for an equilibrium in the game with commitment and in the simultaneous move game. As long as $U_2 \neq 0$, i.e., as long as the external effects are present, then a time consistency problem will exist in this economy. Basically, in the presence of an externality, private agents do not internalize the effects of their wage setting practices on the welfare of others. This leads to an inefficient outcome. Can the government help to deal with this inefficiency?

To answer this question, we need to place some additional restrictions on the preferences of the private agents. These restrictions mirror those that were implicitly imposed in the previous version of this example. First, assume that the best response of the private agents in setting w_i is proportional to π ($\partial w_i / \partial \pi = 1$), reflecting the objectives of agents that their wages grow at the rate of inflation. Second, suppose that $U_3 = 0$ at $\pi = 0$ so that from the perspective of private agents, given real wage growth at the individual and economywide levels, zero inflation is desired.

In the solution with commitment, the government is unable to alter the real wage growth in the economy since variations in π are reflected one-for-one by variations in private wage growth. The optimal policy for the government is simply to set $\pi = 0$, thus avoiding all costs of inflation. Without commitment, once nominal wage growth is set, the government can influence real wage growth, though at a cost since $U_3 = 0$ at $\pi = 0$. The sole incentive for inflation is the presence of an externality: the economywide real wage growth influences the welfare of each wage setter. In equilibrium, the government can never correct this inefficiency: the source of inflation is simply the government's inability to stop itself from trying. The source of inflation is not any divergence in preferences between private agents and the government, though, as noted earlier, this divergence is often sufficient.

Optimal Taxation of Capital and Labor

In this example, which builds upon Fischer [1980], we study the optimal taxation policy of a government. A similar structure underlies the example of multiple equilibria with government intervention introduced earlier in this chapter. Here, though, the stress is on the issue of time consistency rather than the strategic uncertainty alone.

Consider an economy with N private agents and a government. The private agents are active for two periods: saving in youth to finance consumption in old age. The government must finance an exogenously given level of public expenditures from a tax on labor income and a tax on capital income. The issue of time consistency arises from the fact that the government's incentive to tax capital income changes over time. Prior to the savings decision of private agents (period 1), the government recognizes that a high tax on capital income will have an adverse effect on capital accumulation. However, once the savings decisions has been made (period 2), the government has an incentive to tax capital more heavily since it is inelastically supplied. In the absence of a government commitment not to place a high tax on capital income in the second period, private agents will anticipate high taxes and thus reduce savings in the first period. The welfare of private agents will, of course, suffer as a consequence.

More formally, let private agents have preferences described by $U(c_1, c_2, L - n)$ where c_t is period t consumption, L is the endowment of period 2 time and n is the amount worked in period 2. The function $U(\cdot)$ is strictly increasing and strictly concave. Consumption in period 1 is financed by an endowment e of the single commodity that each individual has available in youth. Period 2 consumption is financed by the return from savings in period 1 and the return from working in period 2 less taxes paid to the government. The budget constraints are given by

$$c_1 + s = e \tag{19}$$
$$c_2 = sR(1 - \tau_k) + n(1 - \tau_n)$$

where τ_k is the tax on capital income, τ_n is the tax on labor income and R is the gross return on savings (s).

The government chooses the tax rates to finance a fixed per capita level of expenditures of G. The objective of the government is to maximize the welfare of the representative agent.

First consider the case of commitment. If the government is able to set taxes prior to the savings decision of the agent and is unable to alter these decisions after the choices of the private agents, then the outcome is called the *Ramsey equilibrium*. Let $\tau = (\tau_k, \tau_n)$ be the vector of taxes and denote by $s(\tau)$ and $n(\tau)$ the optimal choices of savings and period 2 labor supply by the representative agent given the tax policy of the government. Further let $V(\tau)$ be the lifetime utility of the agent given the policy τ. With the ability to commit to a tax policy, the government chooses τ to maximize $V(\tau)$ given the response of the private sector to its actions, as summarized by the functions $s(\tau)$ and $n(\tau)$. In this problem, the government faces the constraint of raising sufficient revenues to finance its expenditures as well. Letting U_j be the derivative of the utility function with respect to its jth argument and denoting the multiplier on the government budget constraint by λ, the first-order conditions for the government's problem are given by

$$U_2 sR = \lambda[sR + \tau_k s_k R + \tau_n n_k] \tag{20}$$
$$U_2 n = \lambda[n + \tau_k s_n + \tau_n n_n]$$

where s_j and n_j are the derivatives of the savings and employment decisions to the tax rate on factor $j = k, n$. The allocation with commitment is thus determined implicitly by these two first-order conditions for the government and the choices of individual agents summarized by the two functions, $s(\tau)$ and $n(\tau)$.

Suppose, in contrast to the preceding problem, that the government can alter its taxes after the savings decision has been made but prior to the choice of labor input by the agents. So, we again ask the question, Will the government elect to utilize the policies it chose in the Ramsey equilibrium if the private agents make the same choices too? We shall see that the answer to this question is no, and thus the Ramsey equilibrium is not time consistent.

A theme in the optimal tax literature is that tax rates should be higher as the supply of a good becomes less elastic. That theme reemerges here as the source of time inconsistency. Once savings decisions are made, the stock of capital in period 2 is predetermined and the government has an incentive to raise tax rates on this inelastically supplied input. Thus, if the government could renege on the taxes determined in the solution of the Ramsey equilibrium, then it would do so by raising capital income taxes and lowering labor income taxes. Of course, private agents would recognize this incentive by the government and thus alter their savings behavior. Therefore, once we open the door for the government to reset it taxes, we must, of course, recompute the entire equilibrium.

To see the outcome without precommitment, consider the extensive form in which private agents choose savings, the government selects tax rates and finally the private agents choose employment levels. Working backward, the employment rule of the private sector is given by $n(\tau)$ as before. In the second stage of this game, the government chooses τ to maximize $V(\tau)$ given the level of per capita savings, s, and the function $n(\tau)$. In contrast to the problem with commitment, here there is no response in savings to changes in government policy. The first-order conditions for the government's choice of τ_k and τ_n are

$$U_2 s R = \lambda [s R + \tau_n n_k] \tag{21}$$
$$U_2 n = \lambda [n + \tau_n n_n]$$

Because these two first-order conditions do not include variations in s from changes in the taxes on capital and labor income, the solutions to the two problems (with and without commitment) will be different. In particular, the tax on capital will be higher and the level of savings lower, as we discuss later in more detail. As a consequence, welfare without commitment will be strictly less than welfare with commitment.

A clear example of the difference in outcomes comes from the Chari, Kehoe and Prescott [1989] formulation of this problem. Assume that $U(c_1, c_2, L - n) = u(c_1 + c_2, L - n)$ so that first- and second-period consumption are perfect substitutes. Chari, Kehoe and Prescott show that the Ramsey allocation has $c_1 = 0$ and a capital tax rate of $(R - 1)/R$. At this tax rate, agents are in fact indifferent about their level of saving and are assumed to save their entire period 1 endowment. The remainder of the government revenues are derived from the tax on labor income. To see that this is an optimal tax policy, note that for lower capital income taxes, agents will save their entire endowment so that as the government raises taxes, decisions are not distorted. A tax in excess of $(R - 1)/R$ would yield no revenue at all from savings and is undesirable.

In the absence of commitment, the government has a clear incentive to tax all of the capital income since this is a nondistortionary tax once the savings decision has been made. So, the outcome in the absence of commitment is for the agent to have zero savings, the government to tax all capital income (yielding zero revenue) and the labor income tax to be set to finance government spending. Clearly, this outcome differs dramatically from that with commitment and consumer utility is strictly lower.

Production Complementarities and Government Subsidies

As a final example we consider an economy in which there are strategic complementarities between agents through a production function. In particular, we adopt a variant of the Bryant model in which the level of activity of other agents influences the returns to work by a single agent. Denote by $U(e, E, \pi)$ the payoffs to *choosing* action e when the average level of employment (effort) is E and the current tax policy is denoted by π. The government has two policy variables: a subsidy given by s and a lump sum tax of T so that $\pi = (s, T)$. Assume that the utility of the private agent is linear in consumption,

$$U(e, E, \pi) = f(e)E^\gamma(1 + s) - T - g(e) \tag{22}$$

where $f(e)$ is a strictly increasing, strictly concave production function of the individual's own labor input and $g(e)$ is a strictly increasing, strictly convex disutility of labor function. The influence of the aggregate economy is modeled by E^γ. From this expression for payoffs, note that the subsidy influences the marginal return to work while the lump sum tax has no influence on work incentives because of the linearity assumption.

In the event the government moves first and sets (s, T), private agents would choose employment levels. The Nash equilibrium level of effort by all agents for given government policy is given by

$$f'(e)e^\gamma(1 + s) - g'(e) = 0 \tag{23}$$

Denote the symmetric equilibrium level of effort by $e^*(s)$.[15]

Given $e^*(s)$, the government chooses (s, T) to maximize the utility of

---

15. Assume that $\gamma < ef''(e)/f'(e)$ for all e so that multiple equilibria will not exist.

a representative agent subject to a budget balance constraint that $T = sf(e)e^\gamma$. So revenues equal subsidies in the symmetric Nash equilibrium. The first-order condition for the government's problem is

$$f'(e)e^\gamma + \gamma f(e)e^{\gamma-1} - g'(e) = 0 \tag{24}$$

Using the condition for a Nash equilibrium, this simplifies to

$$\frac{\gamma f(e)}{f'(e)e} = s \tag{25}$$

evaluated at $e = e^*(s)$.

From this condition, the level of the subsidy will be positive when there is a strategic complementarity in the economy, i.e., when $\gamma > 0$. So, when the government has the ability to commit to an action, it will subsidize production to offset the production externality that is not internalized by the private agents. The revenues for this subsidy come from lump sum taxes.

When the government moves after the agents, then the government's choice of (s, T) can have no impact on the employment decisions of the private agents. Once private actions are taken, the welfare of the private agents is independent of the (s, T) selected by the government since these policies simply redistribute goods across the identical agents. If there were any cost to redistribution, such as distortions or resource costs of collected taxes and paying subsidies, then the government would set $s = T = 0$ in the second stage of the game. The private agents would recognize this, and hence the government would be powerless to offset the production externality.

SUMMARY

The point of this chapter was to introduce the government into our analysis of the aggregate economy. Two sources of interaction were described. First, there is the role of the government as a solution to a variety of problems with private allocations arising from the presence of externalities. The extent to which the government can resolve these problems depends on its ability to commit itself to particular actions. In the case of full commitment, we see that the government can act to support efficient outcomes while these allocations may not be achievable when the power to commit is lacking.

Second, we emphasized the role of the government in models with complementarities. Here we see that the government is called upon to play a rather unique role: that of a confidence builder. A theme for much of this book has been coordination failures arising from a crisis of confidence, and thus it is not surprising that a large player, such as a government, can play a positive role in supporting Pareto-efficient equilibria. A leading example is that of deposit insurance, though other forms of government guarantees to, for example, the Chrysler Corporation or the Mexican government have had similar effects of restoring confidence.

The final point is that sometimes the government is a source of rather than a solution to coordination problems. Several examples given here relate to the government's need to balance a budget with exogenously given spending. Thinking of the government as the source of multiplicity has opened up a new area of research for economists interested in macroeconomic complementarities.

8 Concluding Thoughts

The goal of this book is to explore the macroeconomic implications of a particular class of model economies: those built around the presence of complementarities. These models stand in sharp contrast with more standard general equilibrium models, both in their structure and in their implications.

From the perspective of structure, interactions dominated by complementarities provide agents with an incentive to follow the behavior of others. The chapters have been structured to present a wide range of environments in which complementarities naturally emerge.

Informally, economic life is simply different in environments characterized by complementarities. In the usual general equilibrium model, there is a sense that tradeoffs, such as moving along a production possibility frontier, are of primary importance. Here the question is whether we should produce more of some goods at the expense of others. Imbedded in this class of models is a sense of conflict in the interest of the agents: more for one means less for another.

In contrast, models of complementarities are really about life "inside the production possibility frontier." Here there is the distinct possibility for producing more of all goods if activities can be properly coordinated. So conflicting interests can become subordinate to the more general needs of coordination.

In a related way, models with complementarity provide novel insights into economic policy. First, the government can play a major role in supporting confidence in an economy. For many countries, this is seen through the wide range of public guarantee funds, such as those for deposits, pensions, etc.[1] In this way, the government can eliminate Pareto-dominated equilibria. Second, the government may itself be a source of multiplicity, as in the taxation example.

As for implications, the property of complementarity gives rise to the possibility of multiple equilibria as well as the magnification and propagation of shocks. In some settings, the multiple equilibria can be Pareto-ordered, giving specific content to the theme of coordination failure.

This book should be viewed as a progress report of an ongoing research program. The dimensions for further work are rather clear. Thus far, we have a set of environments in which complementarities arise and some, often imprecise, quantification of their magnitude. To keep the material cohesive, we have intentionally ignored the use of models with complementarities for understanding growth as well as the spatial aspects of equilibrium. Clearly these models are structurally quite similar, though the interactions are too often studied independently.

Future work will undoubtedly uncover more sources of complementarity and confront the more difficult question of their quantification. Through this process of model building and testing, these models with complementarities will become an even more useful structure for the evaluation of a large number of economic phenomena.

1. Cooper and Ross [1997] provide an explicit model of guarantee funds in a model with multiple equilibria.

References

Azariadis, C., "Self-Fulfilling Prophecies," *Journal of Economic Theory*, 25 (1981), 380–96.

Ball, L. and D. Romer, "Real Rigidities and the Non-Neutrality of Money," *Review of Economic Studies*, 57 (1990), 183–204.

Barro, R. and D. Gordon, "A Positive Theory of Monetary Policy in a Natural Rate Model," *Journal of Political Economy*, 91 (1983), 589–610.

Basu, S. and J. Fernald, "Are Apparent Productive Spillovers a Figment of Specification Error?" *Journal of Monetary Economics*, 36 (1995), 165–88.

Baxter, M. and R. King, "Productive Externalities and Business Cycles," Institute for Empirical Macroeconomics, Federal Reserve Bank of Minneapolis, Discussion Paper #53, November 1991.

Beaudry, P. and M. Devereux, "Monopolistic Competition, Price Setting and the Effects of Real and Monetary Shocks," mimeo, University of British Columbia, 1993.

Beaudry, P. and A. Guay, "What Do Interest Rates Reveal about the Functioning of Real Business Cycle Models?" mimeo, Université de Montreal, December 1992.

Benassy, J.P., *The Economics of Market Disequilibrium*, New York: Academic Press, 1982.

"Nonclearing Markets: Microeconomic Concepts and Macroeconomic Applications," *Journal of Economic Literature*, 31 (1993a), 732–61.

"Taste for Variety and Optimum Production Patterns in Monopolistic Competition," CEPREMAP, July 1993b.

Benhabib, J. and R. Farmer, "Indeterminacy and Increasing Returns," *Journal of Economic Theory*, 63 (1994), 19–41.

"Indeterminacy and Sunspots in Macroeconomics," mimeo, New York University, 1997.

Blanchard, O. and S. Fischer, *Lectures on Macroeconomics*, Cambridge, MA: MIT Press, 1989.

Blanchard, O. and N. Kiyotaki, "Monopolistic Competition and the Effects of Aggregate Demand," *American Economic Review*, 77 (1987), 647–66.

153

Braun, R. Anton and C. Evans, "Seasonal Solow Residuals and Christmas: A Case for Labor Hoarding and Increasing Returns," Working Paper WP-91-20, Federal Reserve Bank of Chicago, October 1991.

Bryant, J., "A Simple Rational Expectation Keynes-Type Model," *Quarterly Journal of Economics*, 97 (1983), 525–29.

"The Paradox of Thrift, Liquidity Preference and Animal Spirits," *Econometrica*, 55 (1987), 1231–36.

Bulow, J., J. Geanakoplos and P. Klemperer, (1985). "Multimarket Oligopoly: Strategic Substitutes and Complements," *Journal of Political Economy*, Vol. 93, pp. 488–511.

Burnside, C., M. Eichenbaum and S. Rebelo, (1995), "Capital Utilization and Returns to Scale," in Bernanke, B. and Rotemberg, J. (Eds.) *NBER Macroeconomic Annual*, MIT Press: Cambridge, MA: 67–123.

Caballero, R. and E. Engel, "Heterogeneity and Output Fluctuations in a Dynamic Menu-Cost Economy," *Review of Economic Studies*, 60 (1993), 95–119.

Caballero, R. and R. Lyons, "External Effects in U.S. Procyclical Productivity," *Journal of Monetary Economics*, 29 (1992), 209–225.

Cahuc, P. and H. Kempf, "Alternative Time Patterns of Decisions and Dynamic Strategic Interactions," *Economic Journal*, 107 (1997), 1728–41.

Caplin, A. and J. Leahy, "State Dependent Pricing and the Dynamics of Money and Output," *Quarterly Journal of Economics,* 106 (1991), 683–708.

"Business as Usual, Market Crashes and Wisdom after the Fact," *American Economic Review*, 84 (1994), 548–65.

"Aggregation and Optimization with State Dependent Pricing," *Econometrica*, 65 (1997), 601–26.

Carlsson, H. and E. van Damme, "Global Games and Economic Selection," *Econometrica*, 61 (1993), 989–1018.

Chamley, C., "Coordination of Heterogeneous Agents in a Unique Equilibrium with Random Regime Switches," mimeo, Boston University, 1996.

"Social Learning, Delay and Multiple Equilibria," mimeo, Boston University, 1997.

Chamley, C. and D. Gale, "Information Revelation and Strategic Delay in a Model of Investment," *Econometrica*, 62 (1994), 1065–85.

Chari, V.V., P. Kehoe and E. Prescott, "Time Consistency and Policy," in Barro, R. (Ed.), *Modern Business Cycle Theory*, Cambridge, MA: Harvard University Press, 1989.

Chatterjee, S., "Participation Externality as a Source of Coordination Failure in a Competitive Model," mimeo, University of Iowa, 1988.

Chatterjee, S. and R. Cooper, "Entry and Exit, Product Variety and the Business Cycle," NBER Working Paper #4562, December 1993.

Chatterjee, S. and R. Cooper, "Multiplicity of Equilibria and Fluctuations in Dynamic Imperfectly Competitive Economies," *American Economic Review: Papers and Proceedings*, 78 (1988) 353–57.

Chatterjee, S., R. Cooper and B. Ravikumar, "Strategic Complementarity in Business Formation: Aggregate Fluctuations and Sunspot Equilibria," *Review of Economic Studies*, 60 (1993), 795–812.

Christiano, L. and M. Eichenbaum, "Current Real Business Cycle Theories and Aggregate Labor Market Fluctuations," *American Economic Review*, 82 (1992), 430–50.

Ciccone, A. and R. Hall, "Productivity and the Density of Economic Activity," NBER Working Paper #4313, April 1993.

Cooper, R. "Predetermined Wages and Prices and the Impact of Expansionary Government Policy," *Review of Economic Studies*, 57 (1990), 205–14.

"Equilibrium Selection in Imperfectly Competitive Economies with Multiple Equilibria," *Economic Journal*, 104 (1994), 1106–23.

Cooper, R. and D. Corbae, "Financial Fragility and the Great Depression," NBER Working Paper #6094, July 1997.

Cooper, R., D. V. DeJong, R. Forsythe and T. W. Ross, "Communication in the Battle of the Sexes Game," *Rand Journal of Economics*, 20 (1989), 568–87.

"Selection Criteria in Coordination Games," *American Economic Review*, 80 (1990), 218–33.

"Communication in Coordination Games," *Quarterly Journal of Economics*, 107 (1992), 739–71.

"Forward Induction in Coordination Games," *Economics Letters*, 40 (1992), 167–72.

"Forward Induction in the Battle of the Sexes Games," *American Economic Review*, 83 (1993), 1303–16.

"Alternative Institutions for Resolving Coordination Problems: Experimental Evidence on Forward Induction and Preplay Communication," In Friedman, James W. (Ed.), *Problems of Coordination in Economic Activity*, Boston: Kluwer Academic, 1994.

Cooper, R. and J. Ejarque, "Financial Intermediation and the Great Depression: A Multiple Equilibrium Interpretation," *Carnegie-Rochester Conference Series on Public Policy*, 43 (1995), 285–323.

Cooper, R. and J. Haltiwanger, "Inventories and the Propagation of Sectoral Shocks," *American Economic Review*, 80 (1990), 170–90.

"Macroeconomic Implications of Production Bunching: Factor Demand Linkages," *Journal of Monetary Economics*, 30 (1992), 107–28.

"The Macroeconomic Implications of Machine Replacement: Theory and Evidence," *American Economic Review*, 83 (1993a), 360–82.

"Autos and the National Industrial Recovery Act: Evidence on Industry Complementarities," *Quarterly Journal of Economics*, 108 (1993b), 1043–72.

"Evidence on Macroeconomic Complementarities," *REStat*, 77 (1996), 78–93.

Cooper, R., Haltiwanger, J. and L. Power, "Machine Replacement and the Business Cycle: Lumps and Bumps," NBER Working Paper #5260, September 1995, revised 1997.

Cooper, R. and A. John, "Coordinating Coordination Failures in Keynesian Models," *Quarterly Journal of Economics*, 103 (1988), 441–63.

Cooper, R. and A. Johri, "Dynamic Complementarities: A Quantitative Analysis," *Journal of Monetary Economics*, 40 (1997), 97–119.

Cooper, R. and T. Ross, "Bank Runs: Liquidity Costs and Investment Distortions," *Journal of Monetary Economics*, 41 (1998), 27–38.

"Market Fragility and Guarantee Funds: Fundamental and Strategic Uncertainty," ISP Discussion Paper #49, revised 1997.

Crawford, V. "An 'Evolutionary' Interpretation of van Huyck, Battalio and Beil's Experimental Results on Coordination," *Games and Economic Behavior*, 3 (1991), 25–59.

"Adaptive Dynamics in Coordination Games," *Econometrica*, 63 (1995), 103–43.

Dagsvik, J. and B. Jovanovic, "Was the Great Depression a Low-Level Equilibrium?" NBER Working Paper #3726, 1991.

Davis, S. and J. Haltiwanger, "Gross Job Creation and Destruction: Microeconomic Evidence and Macroeconomic Implications," *NBER Macroeconomics Annual*, 1990, 123–86.

"Wage Dispersion between and within U.S. Manufacturing Plants, 1963–1986," *Brookings Papers: Microeconomics*, 1991, 115–200.

"Gross Job Creation, Gross Job Destruction and Employment Reallocation," *Quarterly Journal of Economics*, 107 (1992), 819–64.

Devereux, M., A. Head and B. Lapham, "Exit and Entry, Increasing Returns to Specialization and Business Cycles," mimeo, University of British Columbia, October 1992.

Diamond, P., "Aggregate Demand Management in Search Equilibrium," *Journal of Political Economy*, 90 (1982), 881–94.

and P. Dybvig, "Bank Runs, Deposit Insurance and Liquidity," *Journal of Political Economy*, 91 (1983), 401–19.

and D. Fudenberg, "Rational Expectations Business Cycles in Search Equilibrium," *Journal of Political Economy*, 97 (1989), 606–19.

Dixit, A. and J. Stiglitz, "Monopolistic Competition and Optimum Product Diversity," *American Economic Review*, 67 (1977), 297–308.

Domowitz, I., G. Hubbard and B. Peterson, "Market Structure and Cyclical Fluctuations in U.S. Manufacturing," *Review of Economics and Statistics*, 70 (1988), 55–66.

Durlauf, S., "Multiple Equilibria and Persistence in Aggregate Fluctuations," *American Economic Review*, 81 (1991), 70–74.

"Non-Ergodic Economic Growth," *Review of Economic Studies*, 60 (1993), 349–66.

Eaton, J., "Public Debt Guarantees and Private Capital Flight," *World Bank Economic Review*, 3 (1987), 377–95.

Farmer, R., *The Macroeconomics of Self-Fulfilling Prophecies*, Cambridge, MA: MIT Press, 1993.

Farmer, R. and J. T. Guo, "Real Business Cycles and the Animal Spirits Hypothesis," *Journal of Economic Theory*, 63 (1994), 42–72.

Farrell, J., "Cheap Talk, Coordination, and Entry," *Rand Journal of Economics*, 18 (1987), 34–39.

and G. Saloner, "Standardization, Compatibility, and Innovation," *Rand Journal of Economics*, 16 (1985), 70–83.

Fischer, S., "Dynamic Inconsistency, Cooperation and the Benevolent Dissembling Government," *Journal of Economic Dynamics and Control*, 2 (1980), 93–107.

Friedman, J., "A Review of Refinements, Equilibrium Selection and Repeated Games," in Friedman, James W. (Ed.), *Problems of Coordination in Economic Activity*, Boston: Kluwer Academic Publishers, 1994.

Fudenberg, D. and J. Tirole, *Game Theory*, Cambridge, MA: MIT Press, 1991.

Gale, D., "Dynamic Coordination Games," *Economic Theory*, 5 (1995), 1–18.

"Delay and Cycles," *Review of Economic Studies*, 63 (1996a), 169–98.

"What Have We Learned from Social Learning?" *European Economic Review*, 40 (1996b), 617–28.

Galeotti, M and F. Schiantarelli, "Variable Markups in a Model with Adjustment Costs: Econometric Evidence for U.S. Industry," mimeo, Boston University, July 1991.

Gali, J. "Product Diversity, Endogenous Markups and Development Traps," mimeo, Columbia University, June 1993.

Gali, J. "Monopolistic Competition, Business Cycles, and the Composition of Aggregate Demand," *Journal of Economic Theory*, 63 (1994), 73–96.

González, F. "Individual Experimentation and Aggregate Fluctuations," mimeo, Boston University, 1997.

Guo, J. T. and K. Lansing, "Fiscal Policy, Increasing Returns and Endogenous Fluctuations," mimeo, University of California, Riverside, 1996.

Hall, R. "Market Structure and Macroeconomic Fluctuations," Brookings Papers on Economic Activity, 1986, 285–322.

"The Relationship between Price and Marginal Cost in U.S. Industry," *Journal of Political Economy*, 96 (1988), 921–47.

Booms and Recessions in a Noisy Economy, New Haven, Yale University Press, 1991a.

"Labor Demand, Labor Supply and Employment Volatility," in O. Blanchard and S. Fischer (Eds.), *NBER Macroeconomics Annual,* Cambridge, MA: MIT Press, 1991b.

Haltiwanger, J. and M. Waldman, "Rational Expectations and the Limits of Rationality: An Analysis of Heterogeneity," *American Economic Review*, 75 (1985), 326–40.

Hamilton, J., "A New Approach to the Economic Analysis of Nonstationary Time Series and the Business Cycle" *Econometrica*, 57 (1989), 357–84.

Hammour, M., "Overhead Costs and Economic Fluctuations," mimeo, Columbia University, May 1991.

Hansen, G., "Indivisible Labor and the Business Cycle," *Journal of Monetary Economics*, 16 (1985), 309–27.

Harsanyi, J. and R. Selten, *A General Theory of Equilibrium Selection in Games*, Cambridge: Cambridge University Press, 1988.

Hart, O., "A Model of Imperfect Competition with Keynesian Features," *Quarterly Journal of Economics*, 97 (1982), 109–38.

Heller, W., "Coordination Failure Under Complete Markets with Applications to Effective Demand," in Walter Heller, Ross Starr and David Starrett (Eds.), *Equilibrium Analysis, Essays in Honor of Kenneth J. Arrow*, Vol. II, Cambridge: Cambridge University Press, 1986.

Holmstrom, B., "Moral Hazard in Teams," *Bell Journal of Economics*, 13 (1982), 324–41.

Hopenhayn, H. and R. Rogerson, "Job Turnover and Policy Evaluation in a Model of Industry Equilibrium," mimeo, Stanford University, 1991.

Hornstein, A., "Monopolistic Competition, Increasing Returns to Scale and the Importance of Productivity Shocks," *Journal of Monetary Economics*, 31 (1993), 299–316.

Howitt, P., "Transactions Costs in the Theory of Unemployment," *American Economic Review*, 75 (1985), 88–101.

Howitt, P. and P. McAfee, "Stability of Equilibria with Externalities," *Quarterly Journal of Economics*, 103 (1988), 261–77.

Johri, A., "Search, Money and the Production Decision," mimeo, McMaster University, 1997.

Jones, L. and R. Manuelli, "The Coordination Problem and Equilibrium Theories of Recessions," *American Economic Review*, 82 (1992), 451–71.

Jovanovic, B., "Micro Shocks and Aggregate Risk," *Quarterly Journal of Economics*, 102 (1987), 395–410.

"Observable Implications of Models with Multiple Equilibria," *Econometrica*, 57 (1989), 1431–38.

Kandori, M., G. Mailath and R. Rob, "Learning, Mutation and Long Run Equilibria in Games," *Econometrica*, 61 (1993), 29–56.

Katz, M. and C. Shapiro, "Network Externalities, Competition and Compatibility," *American Economic Review*, 75 (1985), 424–40.

King, R., C. Plosser and S. Rebelo, "Production, Growth and Business Cycles. I. The Basic Neoclassical Model," *Journal of Monetary Economics*, 21 (1988), 195–232.

Kiyotaki, N., "Multiple Expectational Equilibria under Monopolistic Competition," *Quarterly Journal of Economics*, 103 (1988), 695–714.

Kiyotaki, N. and R. Wright, "On Money as a Medium of Exchange," *Journal of Political Economy*, 97 (1989), 927–54.

"A Search Theoretic Approach to Monetary Economics," *American Economic Review*, 83 (1993), 63–77.

Klenow, P., "Externalities and Economic Fluctuations," mimeo, Stanford University, 1990.

Kohlberg, E. and J. Mertens, "On the Strategic Stability of Equilibria," *Econometrica* 54 (1986), 1003–38.

Kydland, F. and E. Prescott, "Rules Rather than Discretion: The Inconsistency of Optimal Plans," *Journal of Political Economy*, 85 (1977), 473–92.

"Time to Build and and Aggregate Fluctuations," *Econometrica*, 50 (1982), 1345–70.

Lam, P., "Permanent Income, Liquidity and Adjustments of Automobile Stocks: Evidence from Panel Data," *Quarterly Journal of Economics*, 106 (1991), 203–30.

Mankiw, N.G., "Small Menu Costs and Large Business Cycles: A Macroeconomic Model of Monopoly," *Quarterly Journal of Economics*, 100 (1985), 529–39.

Maskin, E. and J. Tirole, "A Theory of Dynamic Duopoly. III. Cournot Competition," *European Economic Review*, 31 (1987), 947–68.

"A Theory of Dynamic Oligopoly. I. Overview and Quantity Competition with Large Fixed Costs," *Econometrica*, 56 (1988a), 549–69.

"A Theory of Dynamic Oligopoly. II. Price Competition, Kinked Demand Curves and Edgeworth Cycles," *Econometrica*, 56 (1988b), 570–99.

Milgrom, P. and J. Roberts, "Rationalizability, Learning and Equilibrium in Games with Strategic Complementarities," *Econometrica*, 58 (1990), 1255–78.

Economics, Organization and Management, Englewood Cliffs, NJ: Prentice Hall, 1992.

Murphy, K., A. Shleifer and R. Vishny, "Increasing Returns, Durables and Economic Fluctuations," NBER Working Paper #3014, 1989.

"Building Blocks of Market Clearing Business Cycle Models," *NBER Macroeconomics Annual* 4 (1989), 247–301.

Nash, J., "Non-Cooperative Games," *Annals of Mathematics*, 54 (1951), 286–95.

Obstfeld, M., "Models of Currency Crises with Self-fulfilling Features," *European Economic Review*, 40 (1996), 1037–47.

Pagano, M., "Trading Volume and Asset Liquidity," *Quarterly Journal of Economics*, 104 (1989a), 255–74.

"Endogenous Market Thinness and Stock Market Volatility," *Review of Economic Studies*, 56 (1989b), 269–88.

Persson, T. and G. Tabellini, *Macroeconomic Policy, Credibility and Politics*, London: Harwood, 1990.

(Eds.), *Monetary and Fiscal Policy*, Cambridge, MA: MIT Press, 1994.

Roberts, J., "An Equilibrium Model with Involuntary Unemployment at Flexible Competitive Prices and Wages," *American Economic Review*, 77 (1987), 856–74.

Rotemberg, J. and G. Saloner, "A Supergame-Theoretic Model of Price Wars during Booms," *American Economic Review*, 76 (1986), 390–407.

Rotemberg, J. and M. Woodford, "Cyclical Markups: Theory and Evidence," NBER Working Paper #3534, December 1990.

"Markups and the Business Cycle," paper presented at the NBER Sixth Annual Conference on Macroeconomics, March 1991.

"Oligopolistic Pricing and the Effects of Aggregate Demand on Economic Activity," *Journal of Political Economy*, 100 (1992), 1153–1207.

Schelling, T. C., *The Strategy of Conflict*, Cambridge, MA: Harvard University Press, 1960.

Schmitt-Grohe, S. and M. Uribe, "Balanced Budget Rules, Distortionary Taxes and Aggregate Instability," mimeo, Federal Reserve Board of Governors, 1996.

Shea, J., "Do Supply Curves Slope Up?" *Quarterly Journal of Economics*, 108 (1993), 1–32.

"Complementarities and Comovements," mimeo, University of Wisconsin, 1993.

Shleifer, A., "Implementation Cycles," *Journal of Political Economy*, 94 (1986), 1163–90.

Stokey, N., "Learning by Doing and the Introduction of New Goods," *Journal of Political Economy*, 96 (1988), 701–17.

Stokey, N. and R. Lucas, *Recursive Methods in Economic Dynamics*, Cambridge, MA: Harvard University Press, 1989.

Tarski, A. "A Lattice-Theoretical Fixpoint Theorem and Its Applications," *Pacific Journal of Mathematics*, 5 (1955), 285–308.

Topkis, D., "Minimizing a Submodular Function on a Lattice," *Operations Research*, 26 (1978), 305–21.

"Equilibrium Points in Nonzero-sum *n*-person Submodular Games," *SIAM Journal of Control and Optimization*, 17 (1979), 773–87.

Trejos, A. and R. Wright, "Search, Bargaining, Money and Prices," *Journal of Political Economy*, 103 (1995), 1118–41.

Van Huyck, J., R.C. Battalio and R.O. Beil, "Tacit Coordination Games, Strategic Uncertainty and Coordination Failure," *American Economic Review*, 80 (1990), 234–48.

"Strategic Uncertainty, Equilibrium Selection and Coordination Failure in Average Opinion Games," *Quarterly Journal of Economics*, 106 (1991), 885–910.

"Asset Markets as an Equilibrium Selection Mechanism: Coordination Failure, Game

Form Auctions and Tacit Communication," *Games and Economic Behavior*, 5 (1993), 485–504.

Van Huyck, J., J. Cook and R. Battalio, "Selection Dynamics, Asymptotic Stability and Adaptive Behavior," *Journal of Political Economy*, 102 (1994), 975–1005.

Vives, X., "Nash Equilibrium in Oligopoly Games with Monotone Best Responses," CARESS Working Paper #85-10, University of Pennsylvania, 1985.

"Nash Equilibrium with Strategic Complementarities," *Journal of Mathematical Economics*, 19 (1990), 305–21.

Weil, P., "Increasing Returns and Animal Spirits," *American Economic Review*, 79 (1989), 889–94.

Weitzman, M., "Increasing Returns and the Foundation of Unemployment Theory," *Economic Journal*, 92 (1982), 787–804.

Index